A CELEBRATION
OF FAITH

A CELEBRATION OF FAITH

By

Austin Farrer

HODDER AND STOUGHTON

CONTENTS

EDITOR'S PREFACE

Austin Farrer died on the twenty-ninth of December 1968, at the age of sixty-two. Most of the sermons in this collection come from the last eight years of his life, when he was Warden of Keble College, Oxford, but some belong to the later years of his long period as Chaplain of Trinity College. They show the many-sidedness of his ministry and the perfect wedding in him of theologian and priest.

Gratitude is due to Mrs Farrer for inviting me to construct this book; to his friends and mine for suggesting pieces that I should hunt for; to Professor Basil Mitchell and the Editor of *The Oxford Magazine* for letting me include a slightly adapted version of the address which Professor Mitchell delivered at the memorial service on the first of February 1969 in Keble College Chapel; to the Rev. Christopher Stead, Chaplain of Keble, for contributing the version of *Veni, Creator Spiritus*, whose manuscript he possesses; to Mr Martyn Skinner for permission to quote from *The Return of Arthur*; and to the B.B.C. for permission to print the sermon on The Ultimate Hope, which was broadcast in a service from St Andrew's, Headington, on the twenty-second of December 1968, the Sunday before he died.

Trinity College,   LESLIE HOULDEN
Oxford.

VENI, CREATOR SPIRITUS

Come down, Creator Spirit, find
A harbour in thy people's mind;
With grace celestial consecrate
The heart of clay thou didst create.

Thy very name is Comforter,
The highest gift the skies confer,
The flow of life, the fire, the love,
The unction poured from God above.

Thou Finger stretched from heaven's throne
Whose touch is sevenfold benison;
Thou Promise of the Father, rich
In sudden dower of golden speech;

Infuse our soul with kind desire,
Our senses light with shining fire;
Confirm with lasting hardihood
The cowardice of flesh and blood.

Bring peaceful hours, and banish far
All enmities that augur war.
With such a guide to go before
No hurtful thing can harm us more.

Make through thyself the Father known,
Reveal the person of the Son,
And grant a constant faith, to see
Their Spirit equally in thee.

AUSTIN MARSDEN FARRER

Austin Farrer was, by common consent, one of the most remarkable men of his generation. He possessed the qualities of originality, independence, imagination and intellectual force to a degree amounting to genius, and the word was sometimes used of him. Yet the word has romantic associations with the self-expression of a striking personality which are wholly inappropriate in his case. It is true that everything he did or said bore the stamp of his personality —except that the metaphor suggests the imposition of form upon recalcitrant matter; rather his acts betrayed the man in the way his handwriting did—and there was a strain of fantasy which sometimes took charge. Yet always the intention and the effect was to direct one's gaze away from the man to whatever was the object of *his* attention. There was a kind of transparency about him.

His scholarship was immense, but was never obtruded. Indeed he always avoided the usual apparatus of scholarship. His books had no footnotes and often no index. His intellectual activity was like a flame; the materials which fed it were so efficiently consumed that no residue remained. It was a flame, sometimes fierce, sometimes wayward, but always casting unexpected light.

He used to find it hard to take at all seriously the objections of philosophers to the notion of a pure spirit, and one couldn't help supposing that this was because he himself approximated so closely to that condition.

Slight and spare in build and swift in movement, he flew upstairs and, like a child, wherever he went he almost always ran. The Warden sprinting across two quadrangles from his lodging to the chapel was a sight as familiar to members of this college as it was astonishing to visitors. It sometimes seemed as if he did not continuously occupy space for, if one met him in the town, one moment he was there talking to one on the pavement, and the next he was half way across the street. He was thought to be shy and in a sense he was—he always had difficulty in beginning or ending a conversation

—but he had the rare capacity to be entirely present to a person, especially if that person was in practical difficulty, intellectual perplexity or spiritual distress.

It would be wrong to call him unworldly without qualification. He enjoyed physical activity and was quite unlike the sort of academic who thinks but cannot act. Thought with him was incipient action. He seemed not to suffer the drag of inertia which affects most of us. In matters of administration, if he had a fault, it was that of being too decisive. He was not in the least remote from the world in which cabbages are grown, furniture mended, roofs inspected and drains cleared. In another sense, perhaps, he *was* unworldly. He was almost entirely indifferent to and largely unaffected by the world in which reputations are made, movements initiated, influences received or imparted. Using the word broadly, he had no *political* interests. It was difficult to get him to take seriously the organised activities of any body intermediate between the college and the cosmos. It was entirely natural that in one of his most memorable sermons he should have maintained that the City of God was really a collection of villages.

He might almost have said 'colleges'. For he was a man of deep and local loyalties who could not be understood apart from the places which nurtured him. He was in every way an Oxford man, a product of the Oxford Greats School and the Oxford Theology School; and, if an Oxford man, then a college man. He acknowledged a debt to each of the colleges of which he was a member. Balliol taught him; St Edmund Hall made him a teacher; Trinity mellowed him, and Keble gave him scope. He enjoyed the meeting of young and old which the college made possible and he delighted in the life of an institution in which men of sometimes strikingly different temperament and outlook could work happily together as colleagues.

He would not himself have seen any paradox in the contrast between these strong local attachments and the unrestricted range and scope of his thinking—that utter lack of parochialism in time or space which makes it extraordinarily difficult to *place* him in any survey of contemporary thinkers. He was a man—to use the words of Thomas Traherne—'as familiar with the ways of God in all ages as with his walk and table'. As such he was an embarrassment to those who were anxious to discern trends and to plot correspondences—just as he was, for that matter, to anyone making *any* sort of list; one simply had to name the others and then add, 'And then, of course, there's Austin Farrer.'

He was for the whole of his career an unfashionable thinker, or rather a *non*-fashionable one. As a philosopher he was examining with a fresh eye the fundamental problems of metaphysics at a time when the rest of us either said the thing was impossible or considered ourselves adventurous if we canvassed its possibility. He was a speculative theologian at a time when the world at large had little use for theology and theologians little use for speculation. He wrote always with such wit and grace that there were no visible signs of strain, but it required intellectual and moral courage of a high order to pursue an unwavering course against the dominant currents of the age. He must sometimes have been tempted to withdraw altogether from the stream of contemporary philosophy and to ignore its problems. If so he did not yield to the temptation. 'The grand error about intellectual integrity,' he once wrote, 'is the belief that it can be achieved by limitation of view; by scrupulous care in cleaning out the moat of an ivory tower or cultivating the hedges round a fool's paradise. There can be no integrity about refusing to pronounce upon things from which we avert our eyes. Integrity of mind is the acknowledgement of truth.' He refused to dodge logical difficulties or to let persuasion masquerade as proof, and when he ventured into physics or physiology he made sure he knew what he was talking about.

One had the impression that as he grew older his intellectual and devotional life and his practical activities became steadily more unified and his habitual mode of expression at once more simple and more individual. His concern was increasingly with people, and whether he was exploring the logical problem of analogy or reflecting, as he loved to do, upon the mystery of the Trinity, persons were the clue, and relation between persons the end. There is very little polemic in his writing. He tends to think the thoughts of his critics with them, so that the discourse keeps on falling, quite naturally, into the form of a dialogue, in which both parties contribute to the final elucidation.

The pattern of his thought is seen most clearly in his sermons. They began with some odd or amusing everyday incident, told in a straightforward conversational style. They ended, some ten minutes later, in an inspired invocation of the majesty of God. It was impossible later to remember how the transition had been achieved.

His hearers had been led from the world to God by being enabled to share in the form of his own meditation. There was no attempt to carry them away, no laying siege to the emotions. There was no discernible difference of tone between preaching and lecturing or between lecturing and everyday speech. Even the sustained eloquence of his Bampton Lectures was no more than the natural and unaffected expression of a unified intellectual and spiritual vision. Yet surely St Mary's had seen and heard nothing like it since John Henry Newman occupied that pulpit.

Not long before he died he remarked to a friend that he had done the things he had wanted to do. He had written all the books he had to write, although not all he could write. He had helped to build the reputation of his college; during what remained of his life he would try to be a good man.

It was characteristic of him to state that task so simply. It sounds a modest task set before himself by a modest man. He was indeed a very humble man, but his humility lay not in any belief that only a limited, mild and unexacting task was laid upon him, but in his conviction that nothing less was demanded than the love of God and his fellow men and that only by the grace of God could he attain to that.

BASIL MITCHELL.

I.

For Reason

ON RELIGION, NATURAL AND REVEALED

Hulsean Sermon, preached in Great St Mary's, Cambridge, 1959

The founder of this sermon directed us to consider the excellence of revealed religion. I take it that 'excellence' in his vocabulary meant 'superiority'. He was not asking us, that is, simply to utter encomiums on divine revelation, but to institute a favourable comparison. There was natural religion, and there was revealed religion. Many people said that natural religion was good enough for them; but we were to urge the contrary. We were to display before the eyes of a not sufficiently appreciative public the superior advantage of revealed truth.

In the time of John Hulse, the distinction between natural belief and a faith supernaturally revealed, was familiar. A comparison between the two had been the whole stock-in-trade of Butler's admired *Analogy*, a book which it is easier now to praise than to read. Our trouble is, we find the very idea of natural religion artificial; it smacks of oracular conscience, copybook metaphysics, and the noble savage. One thing at least is clear to us, when we look back on the age of Butler and of Hulse. What was taken by them to be natural religion was deeply indebted to Christian faith. It was supposed to derive from a view of the world and of man, simply as we see them to be. But these natural realities had been looked at so long with Christian eyes, that they had taken on a Christian sort of look. People could not distinguish naked fact from inveterate interpretation. An old man may find it intolerable to revisit his college, because (he says) the staircases are full of ghosts. The ghosts are not there; but he cannot see the walls and banisters, without expecting the footfall of friends long dead. In some such way the vaunted Age of Reason could not see a natural world, unhaunted by the ghost and echo of ancestral faith.

What I have just remarked would be too trite for repetition, if we were proposing to leave it at that. But our historical platitude places us in a situation in which we can scarcely hope to sit down, and

repose. If the old natural theologians were listening to the rever-
berations of a Christian thunder, muttering on among the rocks of
natural fact, we still do not know how we ought to handle the issue
which they too credulously defined. Perhaps the obvious course to
take is that which has commended itself to the austere philosophers.
Banish the Christian echoes, lay the last ghost of positive religion
in any form, strip the facts of nature and of man down to a naked
objectivity, and then see if there is anything of a theological ten-
dency which, in contemplating them, you cannot but believe. If
there is any such inescapable and residual theology, you may speak
of natural religion—not, that is, a religion natural to Hottentots but
a religion natural to that level of mentality and culture, which the
graduates of our more respectable universities have attained.

The project sounds laudable; it positively bristles with intellectual
integrity. Unhappily it is as sterile as it is aseptic. Strip the facts
down to what no one with a head on his shoulders, and eyes in his
head, can dispute, and they will yield you no theology. If you want
any, you will be obliged to let in the ambiguous test: 'What is there
more, which, in contemplating the bare facts, I cannot but believe?'
—or rather, *could* not but believe, under an unreal supposition: the
supposition that I had received no illumination and felt no influence, whether direct or indirect, from any mouthpiece of revealed
truth, or any tradition of positive faith. Unluckily, the proposed
experiment in hypothetical believing is impossible to make. I can
experiment in scientific reasoning, under the artificial condition that
I use no premises introduced into European thought later than
Aristotle. But I cannot experiment in reacting to the realities of my
situation, as I should have reacted if Moses, Buddha, Christ, Augustine, my father, my schoolmaster and my nurse had never opened
their mouths. I can only react as I do react, being the man that I am.
And what man am I? The man that these I have named, among
many others, have made me to be.

Even if, by a miracle, I could do it—could make a reaction to the
world, unaffected by any inspired or revelatory utterances ever
given—it is still not clear what the value of such a reaction would
be. For we commonly think that, whatever the great prophets and
revealers have or have not done, they have brightened, purified and
refined our reaction to nature and to life. If there can be said to be
such a thing as a true and proper response of the heart and will to
this shared human existence of ours, and to its several situations,

will a man be more capable of it who has learned nothing from Christ, and nothing from Buddha? In looking for natural religion, as we said, we are not looking for the religion of Esquimaux and Hottentots: we are looking for something which results from the unbiased use of civilised faculties. But civilised faculties, like civilisation itself, are a historical product; and the history which produces spiritual faculty is spiritual history; a history in which Christ, the Buddha and others we have named or not named, play decisive parts.

What follows from the considerations we have advanced? Are we to conclude that the eighteenth-century distinction between natural and revealed religion was meaningless? We should be rash to conclude so, without first hearing the defence of those we criticise.—But the men are dead.—Never mind: since we have talked of ghosts, let us raise a ghost: let us pose our eighteenth-century deist with our twentieth-century question. I bar table-rapping; I propose straight mediumship, and I offer myself as the medium. Listen, then, to the voice of a spirit in a powdered wig.

'You tell me, Sir,' says he, 'that what I took to be the mere motions of our rational nature are an acquired habitude, which the prophets and lawgivers of former generations have largely formed in us; that because we look as they have taught us to look, we see what they have instructed us to see. I will be so candid as to confess, that your arguments convince me on this head. And indeed it must be acknowledged more in general, that the powers of our human nature attain neither maturity nor use, without teachers to cultivate and to develop them. I myself, in the idleness of my youth, amused many hours with drawing and painting; and for such poor skill as I had, was entirely indebted to several masters. They taught my eye to distinguish a beauty in the scenes of nature, and my pencil to delineate it. Yes, Sir, they taught me; for (not to flatter myself) I was not born unteachable. But here lies the point—they taught *me* to see, and *me* to draw. They taught me not what they saw, nor what they drew; they taught me to draw, and to see; and it was by my own acquirements that I measured the value of their instructions. They had several theories and systems, some of which seemed to me fantastical, and all superfluous, except as they served to foster in me the pictorial art. All was but scaffolding to raise a house. The house once finished, the scaffolding is carted away, and no more accounted of.

'Now, Sir, I will confess that the sages and, since you will have it
so, the prophets of former times, have taught me to think, to feel,
and to act. Very well; I will do these things, and I will thank them
for the ability. I will use my faculties to the best of my powers, and
reason as I may on what I perceive. But I will not trammel myself
in the systems of ancient philosophers, or in the visionary meta-
physick of the prophets. Indeed, I will propose to you a pragmatic
test for distinguishing the grain of antiquity from the chaff. Whatsoever in these old oracular teachings has become, as it were, incorporate with our faculties, and passed into the very ideas we have
of the objects about us, so much is of worth; the rest is nothing to
us. The teachings of antiquity have been called the food of the
mind. But I will beg leave to observe, that the evidence of nourish-
ment lies in the assimilation of it. What passes into our physical
being is food. What does not is at the best an encumbrance, at the
worst, a poison.'

Return, Alphaeus; the dread voice is past . . . our deistical ghost
vanishes as suddenly as he came. But surely he has left us something to think about. Has he not expressed, with the hard clarity of
the Age of Reason, a view more vaguely and less consciously held by
many of ourselves? Christianity, such people will generously admit,
has given us new eyes for the qualities and claims of personal existence: qualities so rich and claims so stringent, that we cannot but
take them for the gifts of an infinite bounty, and the requirements
of an absolute will. We may refresh the Christian lesson, and kindle
anew our perception for these things by reading the Gospels. But
we can make no approach to reality save by throwing ourselves upon
these things. We cannot know God or his will save as we find him
expressed in the beings we encounter; in their virtues, their needs,
their potentialities, their aspirations. Or if we can know more of
him, it is not through any record of the past; it is by a direct wrestling with an ever-present eternity in the difficult practice of mystical
contemplation.

Such, we may fairly say, is the general shape of a natural religion
widely prevalent. How many people do we know, who honour
Christ and repudiate atheism, but believe no supernatural creed,
no mystery accepted on the credit of any revealer? And the first
thing we are moved to say about their religion is, that there is much
virtue in it. What a refreshing contrast it offers to much, if not most,
dogmatic belief! Do we not approach the fully-practising, orthodox

Christian with the sickening fear that we shall find a being prejudiced and profoundly insincere, unwilling to trust his eyes, his
reason or his heart, anxiously substituting a world of cardboard
maxims, for the glorious and terrifying universe which God has
made? How infinitely more wholesome the lapsed but unresentful
Catholic, still instinct with natural reverence, while his heart beats
freely in a blessed new release from believing things other than
they seem!

I am put up here to preach the excellence of revealed religion, so
I must not allow the beautiful candour of natural piety to carry me
quite away. But I will say that unless the virtues of natural religion
find a place in the life of orthodoxy, orthodoxy becomes the carica-
ture of itself, and the bugbear of honest minds.

> Hail, holy light, offspring of Heaven first born!
> Or of the Eternal co-eternal beam
> May I express thee unblamed? Since God is light,
> And never but in unapproachèd light
> Dwelt from eternity—

and in his light we are to see light.
The evidence of light is that it illuminates; and if by the light of
faith we do not see more colours in the world, more exactly in their
proper being and truth, than eyes can perceive which lack supernatural illumination, then surely we stand self-condemned.

The Christian mind must move in equipoise between revealed
mysteries and open realities, interpreting each by the help of the
other; as happens very simply and without our observing it, when
we join the adoration of God's goodness with the prayerful remem-
brance of our friends. But of course there is no equality between
our two objects of contemplation; and though the glory of the
divine countenance is reflected in the looking-glass of creatures, it
is not, and cannot be, all reflected there. Thus the resolution to see
nothing of God, but what is given back to our eyes by the creaturely
mirror, is a resolution to leave out most of what there is to be seen.
And, formally speaking, the superiority or excellence of revealed
religion is precisely this: it tells of the special means God has taken
to show us, outside the common course of nature, some part of that
great overplus, which exceeds the capacity of nature's looking-glass
to reflect it.

It is not even as though what natural fact does show of God were self-explanatory or self-contained. Perhaps the liveliest part of natural religion is a sensitivity to the will of God, as it comes home to us in the needs or the aspirations of our fellow-men. Yet we cannot see what their needs are, unless we know what they need to be; nor how to support their aspirations, without a vision of their goal, a goal so widely misconceived. Or again, how shall we relate the pure will of God to the perverse strivings of men, without an understanding of the atonement which forgives them, or the grace which reclaims and rectifies them?

If we are possessed by revealed truth, and not merely encumbered by credal diagrams of it, it will not deaden, it must enliven our sensitivity to present personal fact. So supernatural light strengthens the beam of natural understanding. 'I am the light of the world,' says Christ in these autumn days, when night begins to crowd upon the year. And, in support of the claim, when they challenge it, 'I know whence I came, and whither I go. You, not knowing whence I come, nor yet whither I go, judge according to the flesh,' by a judgement, that is, no more than natural. For without the disclosure of our goal and our origin, how can we discern the straight from the crooked in the paths of life? It is one thing to walk from the womb in pursuit of a utopia which flees us; another thing, issuing from the hand of God, to walk towards a Mercy who comes to meet us. And what is a straight walk, on the first view, may be a very crooked walk on the second.

For a Christian, there is something absurd about the invitation to proclaim the superiority of revealed religion—to argue that we are better off with the light, the grace and the glory, the quickening water and the redeeming blood, than we should be without these things. That they are excellent, who can doubt, if only he believes them? And if there is one cause of disbelief most endemic to the natural religion we have discussed, it is probably the notorious 'scandal of particularity'—the apparent preposterousness of letting any particular set of events bear the unique importance which Christ's intervention bears for the Christian. How can Jesus have done more than heighten the perceptiveness with which we survey facts in general, and especially personal facts?

Since I cannot hope, in the last sentences of a sermon, to say anything useful in mitigation of the scandal of particularity, I will stand down once more, and give place to a more persuasive voice.

In the last published part of Martyn Skinner's astonishing poem, *The Return of Arthur*, an unbeliever finds himself entranced in a church, gazing at a wooden plaque of the Nativity.

So Leo gazed, absorbed, a timeless glance;
And thought of all the trees that nature held
(Strange instance of a trance within a trance);
Cedars of Lebanon, green beechwoods delled
With sapphire; sombre newsprint forests felled
 At such a rate, each Sunday men were able
 To read ten acres at the breakfast table;

Dwarf fairy oaks at Lichen, harled with moss;
Trunks wide as roads, through which a cart could go;
A jungle mat a continent across
Which, piled as logs, would make the Alps look low—
And yet of all that ever grew, or grow
 (So ran his thoughts) this carving had been done
 Uniquely from a random plank of one.

Was not the contrast much the same in space,
Whose glittering forests were the galaxies?
For if the carver made a special case,
Selecting from innumerable trees
One segment, so from the vast host of these
 Could not the prime Creator, mightier far,
 Have carved his story on a single star?

And if he had, Ah, if indeed he had,
And come himself to earth, a newborn cry,
Would not the story have been just like that;
And signs accompanied, in earth and sky,
That holy abdication from on high;
 And radiant beings from about the throne
 Of Light, have made the lamplit stable known?

Now therefore to the Light of light, the threefold fountain both of being and of grace, Father, Son and Holy Ghost . . .

DOUBLE THINKING

It is a very ancient and mossy platitude, that men throw away price-less opportunities for self-improvement by resenting criticism instead of taking it to heart. And what is true of men is true of doctrines and systems. If only we could seriously consider what the communists say about us, instead of blasting them with cries of 'You're another!' And if only the Church in every age had been as concerned to see what had driven the heretics into heresy, as she was to condemn and suppress them! For the heretics were as serious men as the orthodox, often more serious. Well, it is easy to be wise after the event: our fathers burnt the heretics and we touch up the crests on the Martyrs' Memorial. But cannot we, in our own time, show a little more wisdom and listen seriously to our own heretics?

Two nights ago I was so rash as to let myself be put up in a sort of public match or verbal cock-fight with an unbelieving philosopher. He was to attack theology, I was to defend it. Neither of the birds (needless to say) achieved a kill. I had heard all the arguments before: so, I expect, had he. He argued kindly and temperately. He had no need to get excited, he was so entirely convinced of his own position. But how strange it is, that two men so different inside should present the same placid face to one another, and exchange little neat verbal arguments about the two different universes in which they respectively live! There is no God in his world: he has yet to be convinced that belief in God has any serious meaning or can be discussed on a respectable level. Whereas I—I, like you, make it a rule to spend a certain part of every day conversing with this God, whom my fellow philosopher more than suspects of not existing. I put a good part of my available nervous energy and a fixed ratio of my time into the endeavour to hold my existence in a focus which is for him a spot of moonshine.

Meanwhile, a room full of young philosophers or would-be philosophers watch the cock-fight. If they took it seriously, I suppose their world ought to turn upside down with every apparent

swaying of the battle. Fortunately, the young men don't take
argumentative dons as seriously as that.

But I must take seriously what my colleague thinks: not, that is,
to call my faith in doubt, for since God has shown to me a ray of his
goodness, I cannot doubt him on the ground that someone has
made up some new logical puzzles about him. It is too late in the
day to tell me that God does not exist, the God with whom I have
so long conversed, and whom I have seen active in several living
men of real sanctity, not to mention the canonised saints. But there
must be much in our teaching of Christianity and our living of it
which is at fault, if good men react in total disbelief of it. So let us
open our ears to what they say, and take the implied criticism to
heart. This Chapel is no place in which to argue against the unbelieving philosophers: it would be ungenerous, for this is not a
place where they can argue back. But this is a fine place in which to
take their criticisms to ourselves, and examine our own consciences.

Let us take, for example, the accusation of 'double thinking' which
is brought against us Christians. Allow me to remind you how that
accusation comes in. You have to suppose first that the critical
philosopher has proved to his own satisfaction that religious beliefs
can have no meaning at all in terms of real life. Religious beliefs and
ceremonies are just superfluous decorations. In fact all religion in a
scientific age is fundamentally of the same character as the religion
practised by a couple of sentimental atheists getting married in
church because it sounds more comforting. But, you and I object,
we are not sentimental atheists: we really do believe. To which the
answer is given: You *think* you believe; but you are deceived. You
are a double thinker: you have two systems of thinking which in fact
you keep apart—you think, as people say, in watertight compart-
ments. And when you switch from one system of your thinking to
another, that is, from your religious thinking to your practical
thinking, you turn a blind eye to the transition, the passage from the
world of reality to the world of fantasy. In the world of reality you
think like anyone else (unless, of course, you are a lunatic or a
fanatic). But when you turn to your devotions, or read pious books,
you enjoy a fantasy picture of the world as subject to God's goodness
and governed by his providence. And in this fantasy picture of the
world there is a fantasy picture of yourself as a Christian, mysteriously incorporate with Christ and serving his cause, with only
occasional lapses and deviations. Whereas in fact you are just an

undergraduate or a business man, or some other type of worldly man, a serious man, perhaps a virtuous man, but one who does not take the will of God into his practical calculations, or experience his life as conducted by God. That is just a story you amuse yourself with while you are worshipping or praying or talking pious talk.

Well, now I think you will see what the accusation of double thinking amounts to: and I think also that you will see how deeply the accusation bites into our consciences, and how important it is that we should lay it to heart. For which of us Christians is there, whose conscience does not reproach him bitterly with the crime of double thinking, or, as Christ himself called it, the crime of hypocrisy? For hypocrisy, as attacked by Christ, does not mean self-conscious humbug, it means just 'play acting', that is to say, that the religion of the hypocrite no more enters into the rest of his life than the part the player acts on the stage enters into his life off the stage. In fact, Christ meant by hypocrisy what is now called 'double thinking', the endemic disease of religion everywhere.

Notice that our critics make the substance of religion what we reject as the vice of religion and its most deadly poison. How does this come about? Are not we the men who have brought it about? Am I not, perhaps, the Christian don who is just like any unbelieving don, except that I sometimes talk theology for professional reasons? And are not you, perhaps, the undergraduate who is just like any other unbelieving undergraduate, and proud to be, and whom no one would suspect of being a Christian unless they found you in Chapel? Are we just as ready as anyone else to join in the enjoyable game of slander (called gossip), just as determined as anyone else to make our worldly fortunes, whatever the needs of the Church or of unfortunate men may be? I could go on making up a lot more unpleasant questions like this, but I will forbear.

To return to the main point. To the clever logicians, Christianity is an amiable and harmless hypocrisy. But we take the thing more seriously. Christian hypocrisy is not amiable or harmless at all. We are all hypocrites, indeed, because we are all sinners, but God is saving us out of our hypocrisy, if we are faithful to him: he is forcing the two parts of our thinking together. That is the whole issue in the religious life, not to be a double thinker, or anyhow, to be less and less of one.

It is obvious that our blessed Saviour was not a double thinker at all. He just lived God, or God lived him, it does not matter which we say, though the second is better—I mean, that God lived him. And I have known some men—living men, breathing with us a common air, men with whom I have talked and worked—who were single-minded Christians and simply followed the will of God step by step in this life, without any seeming regard for their own fortune or happiness or life, even. But what visible happiness God gave them in this world! and what happiness he has given them in that other world, eye has not seen, nor ear heard, nor has it entered into the heart of man once to conceive the least part of it.

When the logicians say that there is a certain inevitable division between spiritual thinking and natural thinking, they are in a certain sense right. We can't reconcile the spiritual picture of things and the everyday picture of things completely on the intellectual level. If we claimed to be able to do it, we should claim to comprehend the ways of God as well as we comprehend the ways of this world, and that would be an exaggerated claim. We see God in pictures, in images only, reflected in a glass and riddlingly says St Paul: and we cannot fuse our picture of God perfectly with our picture of the natural world. There always remains a certain discontinuity, a certain incoherence on the intellectual level.

The saints confute the logicians, but they do not confute them by logic but by sanctity. They do not prove the real connection between the religious symbols and the everyday realities by logical demonstration, but by life. *Solvitur ambulando*, said someone about Zeno's paradox, which proves the impossibility of physical motion. It is solved by walking. *Solvitur immolando*, says the saint, about the paradox of the logicians. It is solved by sacrifice. I can offer my life to the God who has shown me his face in the glass of riddles. The God who is seen in the sphere of religion takes control in the sphere of conduct, and there he gives me, unworthy, the help of his holy spirit.

You can live your religion if you like; you can know the reality of God if you like: for God will rejoice to assist and infinitely over-reward whatever effort you will make. *Resolution* is the crucial point. That is the link by which religious contemplation passes into practical action. From your prayers form simple resolutions—not, like the absurd resolutions of New Year's Day, resolutions for the next twelve months; but resolutions for the next twelve hours. Make them few enough to be practicable, and obey them for the sake of God himself. If you break them, repeat and renew them. What does

God ask of me? is a part of every sincere prayer. By resolutions kept, men turn religious fantasy into the substance of living. By resolutions broken, men learn their weakness and are driven back on God. By resolutions renewed and kept they learn to live by him who says: 'my strength is made perfect in weakness' and 'my grace is sufficient for thee.'

EMPTYING OUT THE SENSE

I Cor. ii,9.   *Eye hath not seen, nor ear heard,*
it hath not come over the heart of men
what God prepares for them that love him.

I was being told the other day about a former Principal of Brasenose who preached to his College once in twelve months, and this is how he would begin: 'The Greek word *allotrioepiskopos*, as I was saying last year', and so on. It is almost as foolish for me to go on where I left off a month ago, for which of you is going to remember? After all, you are not proposing to do a schools paper on your chaplain's sermons. Nevertheless, I shall commit this absurdity, because we hit on a good vein a month ago, but we did not properly exploit it: so it seems a good plan to revisit the site and see if we cannot dig something more out of it.

The idea, if you remember (but of course you don't) was this. The unbelieving philosophers have been putting up a powerful line of criticism lately against our Christian beliefs, and it seemed that we ought to see what light their criticisms cast either on our beliefs or on our unworthy way of holding our beliefs. We found, for one thing, that they supposed us to be double thinkers, that is, to think one thing on our knees, and something quite different on our feet: and we had to agree that this was only too true, and we spent the sermon reflecting upon that most insidious spiritual disease of double thought. Today we will take up another point of accusation, of which the title is not 'double thinking' but 'emptying-out'.

The point about 'emptying-out' arises like this. You must imagine a theologian—it might be your unfortunate chaplain himself—brought to bay by a ring of savage and keen-scented logicians. 'You say' (thus they begin to bark at him) 'that God is active for your good, that his love makes all things work together for your advantage. But the other day your bicycle skidded and threw you against the wall of a house, and bruised you properly; and today you suddenly got an idea into your head and forgot an important engagement in consequence. Was divine benevolence making the bicycle work for your good when it skidded, or what you call your memory work for your good when it failed you so humiliatingly?' I begin to feel unhappy under such questioning, but (I say) God does work everything for my good, but not in the simple way you seem to expect. He is a very subtle worker, and we cannot always see what sort of good he will achieve for us by his management of events. 'Ah,' the philosophical critics reply, 'God's management of events seems to be management in a highly special sense, almost a Pickwickian sense, mightn't we say? It isn't much like the sort of management we would expect from a good human manager who was really in control. A human traffic manager, for example, who (to suppose the absurd) happened also to be omnipotent, would eliminate nasty accidents. But it appears that God does not do so, either for those who love him, or for those who do not. Some prayer books contain forms for blessing cars; but you do not, I take it, suppose that the proportion of accidents in blessed cars is lower than in those unblessed?' No, I hasten to assure them that I do not suppose anything of the kind. Perhaps, as a matter of fact, I do not hold much of an opinion of the blessing of vehicles. There is a good deal of rust in my car: but none of it is due to the sprinkling of holy water.

'Where, then,' they reply, 'is your alleged faith in providence?' I look down my nose, and wonder how much longer this ordeal is to last, and I say, 'My believing in providence means that whatever happens it will be all right: not that one thing will happen rather than another.' 'Then why,' they retort, 'call it a faith in providence, governance, or management? The words sounded quite full-blooded and real when you began, but in the course of discussion you have been emptying the sense out of them bit by bit, until there is no more meaning left: or if there are still a few drops in the bottom of the cup, we could make you empty them out too, if we pressed you a little longer.'

Now I think we have sufficiently recalled what is meant by the accusation of 'emptying-out'. It means that religious language sounds quite full-blooded and ordinary, but when you press the religious believers they empty more and more of the meaning away, until they seem to be saying nothing at all.

Well, I did not do very well against the logicians, because they got me rattled, but you are my kind friends and fellow-Christians so I will relax and take a deep breath and try to explain myself a bit better. After all, it never was much good trying to explain spiritual things to unbelieving men. When I say unbelieving men, I don't mean humble enquirers, whose hearts God has touched. That is another thing.

Well then, about 'emptying-out'. God wants to give us the best thing in the world, a perfect and supernatural good. How is he going to make it known to us? He has to talk to us in the language we already know, the language of earthly things. If he talked to us the language of heaven, how would we ever understand? God takes our words, and uses them: Jesus spoke the dialect of the Galilean peasantry. Inevitably, the earthly words do not fit the heavenly things. The result is a good deal of initial confusion and disappointment. When we begin to learn our religion, we are told that God will answer us in our prayers: that sounds like the promise of a conversation. But when we try to pray, of course we find it is not like that. And how God's Spirit does touch us in our prayers, is a thing no number of words can properly describe beforehand: only God himself can show us that, if we go on faithfully in our prayers, until we find out something of what it is.

Or again, we are promised happiness in our religion. We soon learn to see that we are not assured by religion of the external means to happiness, such as health and wealth. But we may still expect emotional contentment, peace of mind. Yet even these things are not assured to us in the common sense of the words. The greater the saint, the more he feels the burden of the world's suffering and of his own sin: and yet (most strange) in his very suffering, in the opening of his heart to every assault, he is most blessed so.

What shall we say, then? Are the words 'converse' as applied to prayer or 'happiness' as applied to sanctity emptied out by God's actual dealings with men? Emptied out? Are the words emptied out? What was it Christ said of the words of the ancient law? I came not to dissolve but to fulfil. Not to dissolve, to melt away, to empty of sense, but to fulfil, to make full, to pack with all the meaning they could bear.

God promised many things to the Israelites in their ancient religion, things which seemed as human and literal as the promises we give in his name to Christian children now. If they would be good, they should be blest. His presence should go with them, and defend them from their enemies. Their cause was the winning cause, for he was almighty, and in his name they should rule the world.

The Israelite nation outgrew the religion of childhood, but did they pass off the promises of God with bland philosophic indifference? They did not. They adhered to the promises of God, they were crucified upon the promises of God, and in that national crucifixion they crucified the literal sense of the promises in order that God might reveal to them the true and spiritual sense.

The discarding of the literal sense of God's promises is a trivial jest to the unbelieving philosophers, but to us it is nothing less than the crucifixion of Christ. Perhaps that is why we could not answer the philosophers: for how could one say in such a company, 'That's the issue you are talking about: you are talking about the crucifixion of Christ'? Christ did not take the promises of God to be a jest, because they could not be literally fulfilled. He did not say 'In the face of Roman power we can found no messianic kingdom here'. He said: 'In the face of Roman power, which excludes our messianic kingdom in the literal sense, we will see what sort of messianic kingdom God will make.' He kept the words, and God changed the thing, and so we still call him Christ, Messiah, King, but not in the pre-crucifixion sense. He kept the words; and when Caiaphas asked him, 'Art thou the Christ?' he said, 'I am'; and when Pilate asked him if he were King of the Jews, he did not deny. But God changed the thing. The body of Jesus, first living, then dead, was trussed up and crucified as the Guy of literal messiahship, but God placed his true Messiah on the throne of heaven and in the hearts of his believers.

Well, they say, we empty out the professions of our religious faith. And I suppose we do. Not only do we give away too much in debate with the philosophers: we empty away too much in our own minds, we are content to think that God promises us something or other which is good, but there is no need to press very closely the sense of the words in which he gave his promises to us. Not so Christ: he pressed the sense of the words, those words 'Messiah' and 'kingdom' for example, he pressed them so, that he ran them clean through his heart; and that was how he discovered what they meant, both for himself and for all mankind. He did not empty out the meaning of the words, he lived it out, and found it wonderful; he died for it and found it transfiguring. His fulfilling of the words was not a matter of scholastic exposition, but of death and resurrection.

There is no short cut to the understanding of God's promises. You cannot do it by the wisdom of this world, or by logical sleight of hand. You can do it by active faith alone, by believing in God who has promised, by persevering in purity of life, in constant prayer, in Christ's sacraments, in obedience to every showing of God's will. Then God will reveal to you his excellent things. For, says Christ's apostle, when in the wisdom of God the world failed by wisdom to know God, it pleased God by the folly of the gospel to save believers. Not but that we speak a wisdom among the fully grown, but a wisdom not of this world, nor of the princes of this world who came to naught. But we speak God's wisdom in mystery, the hidden wisdom which God appointed before the ages for our glory; which none of the princes of this age understood, for had they understood, they would not have crucified the Lord of Glory: but as it is written, what eye hath not seen nor ear heard, what hath not come over the heart of man, the provision God had made for them that love him. And our Saviour says, 'I thank thee Father, Lord of heaven and earth, that thou hast hidden these things from the wise and prudent and hast revealed them to babes, for so it seemed good in thy sight.'

HISTORY AND THE GOSPEL

Hulsean Sermon, preached in Great St Mary's, Cambridge, 1948

The Word became flesh, and invisible God was made visible. Therefore the Christian faith is grounded in plain history. The conditions of this Sermon allow the evidences of Christianity to be the preacher's subject, and it is of historical evidences that I propose to speak. I propose to speak of them more in general than in particular. As to the particular points of historical fact which together establish Christian origins, the students of positive theology sift them with learned care; and it is the especial pride and just glory of your theological faculty here, that it has devoted itself to the plain historical and positive method of enquiry. Suppose we desire to know what part of the Christian gospel came from the lips of Christ himself, and what part was supplied by the Spirit of Pentecost speaking in the Apostles; suppose we are concerned to establish the legal and political facts of our Redeemer's condemnation and crucifixion, or the supernatural fact of his resurrection: then we must submit to the rigours of long and exact historical study; there are no short cuts, and nothing which I could summarise here in half an hour would be of any solid use. But even in half an hour we can reflect profitably on the true nature of historical enquiry, and of its particular bearing on the New Testament.

A man's philosophy of history increases in practical importance in proportion as his field of historical study is more obscure. If the field of study is straightforward and well documented, if, for example, the subject is mundane and intelligible, say the biography of a hard-headed politician; and if the period is recent and readily imaginable, say the reign of Queen Victoria; and if the evidences are sufficient, the official papers, the private letters, the garrulous diaries, and the columns of *The Times*: under such conditions as these, the capable historian will make a tolerable job of his undertaking, whatever his doctrine of historical method may be. And if we treat cases of this sort as typical, we shall be likely to conclude that the question of historical method is academic. It may amuse the wits of the philosophers, but it will not affect the practice of the historians.

But we need only choose different instances, and we shall form a different estimate. If we turn from the hard calculations of worldly statecraft to the delicately balanced psychology of religious exaltation; if we leave the English politician for the Jewish saint, and the comfortable familiarity of Victorian London for the twilight strangeness of a Galilean religious underworld, where lost sects and forgotten racial groups touched in the shadow of the synagogue; if we exchange official minutes and dated letters for scraps of sacred legend, and pages of liturgical recitation: faced with materials of this kind, a context of this kind, and questions of this kind, we shall soon be invoking whatever aid and guidance the theory of historic method can bestow.

If there is any historian to whom the theory of his art is of crucial importance, it is the New Testament historian, because his subject-matter is pre-eminently difficult. Yet we do not find that historical theologians have been forward to study the theory of history at a philosophical level. What we do find is that they have been the frequent victims of philosophical propaganda, and the fervent advocates of ready-made methodological recipes. If theologians are specially liable to such intellectual disorders, it will be the effect of the special difficulties inherent in their study. Theologians grasp at a method, as a drowning man grasps at a straw.

When I was a lad we were devoted to the method of documentary analysis; we divided our ancient books into an infinite number of distinct constituents; and the masterpiece of skill was to discover six sources in a paragraph where others had detected only three. When I was a young man, we had thought of something else: we shifted our attention from the documents to the supposed underlying oral traditions, and these we subjected to examination by the somewhat fitful light of a general concept of folk tradition and of its evolution. And now that I have finished growing up, I hear it said that there is a newer and shorter way with the evangelists, called the typological method; but I cannot find out clearly what it is supposed to be, nor who are the authors and protagonists of it.

The first principle of true historical method is to have no method at all, that is, no set and ready-made method. The subject-matter of history is human action, and human action is not, in the last account, studied by a method: it is the object of direct personal understanding.

I say 'in the last account', because set methods offer us assistance in coming to grips with our objective: empirical psychology, for example, and speculative economics may have their parts to play. But ultimate historical reality is human action, and human action can in the end be understood by nothing but personal understanding. As we understand our friend by the direct and sympathetic interpretation of the intention which his words and acts express, so in the end we have got to understand the mind of the characters in our history, or we have understood nothing. From their expressive acts, however indirectly reported to us, we have got to seize *them*. There are indeed regions of history in which we get no further than generalisation, we talk about fictions like 'nation' and 'policy-trend', and never reach the individual at all. But whichever those regions of historical study may be, the study of Christian origin is not among them. We do not want to know statistical averages, we want to know Christ.

Human intentional action is personal and unique. We do not understand our friend's actions as just human actions, but as his actions. It is the element of the unique in human behaviour which makes it impossible to adhere rigidly to any set historical method. There is no method for dealing with the unique: it has just got to be appreciated for what it is. No historical generalisation is more than a pointer to the direction in which unique personal truth may be found to lie. We are always well advised to look, but never certain to find, along the line indicated. It may be true in general, for example, that a despot in difficulties at home will wish to shake them off by foreign war. But if there is a despot in our own world girt with domestic difficulties of the sort which have impelled other despots to war, it is still not certain that he welcomes the prospect of international conflict, or that his apparent efforts to avert it are insincere and intended to fail. It may be so, or it may not be so; we could only judge (which, in the case of a contemporary, is scarcely possible to any but his intimates) by piecing the man together out of all our evidence about him, both in the present crisis of his statecraft and in the rest of his life, and then seeing what he is up to. We cannot go by his utterances alone, for in any case they conflict. In some he was lying, in others perhaps revealing himself. But in which? We can only understand him in terms of all the evidence about him; and the evidence about him in terms of himself.

If the unique is in history at all, it is in Christ. Yet only consider the sway of stale generalisations in the interpretation of him! Who, for example, can estimate the influence which has been exercised by the banal maxim: 'Religious pioneers do not preach their own divine function, they preach a saving way. It is their followers who divinise them for having preached it.' How many scholars have written with this axiom in their minds, and used it as a criterion in sifting the scriptural evidence? According to the Gospels, Christ was the supernatural regent of God's kingdom, and he was to be crucified. Therefore he said to his disciples, 'He that would save his life must forfeit it': the sacrifice of Messiah must include that of his followers. That is what the Gospels say; but our cherished axiom says otherwise: the principle of dying to live must have been preached as a universal moral truth, illustrated indeed by the death of Christ, but in principle independent of it. It is not, then, because Messiah loses his life to gain it that his followers are involved in sacrifice. They are involved in it because they are men, and sacrifice is the law of man's condition. On an impartial view of the historical evidence, there is nothing to be said for this opinion—nothing to be said for the hypothesis that the Christian gospel was first a general doctrine of self-sacrifice, and only later centred on the sacrifice of Christ. The only ground for saying anything so perverse is prejudice. We think that a flat and not very well-grounded generalisation about religious pioneers must be true of Christ, and our estimate of the evidence falls into line.

In truth the historian who views Christ as a religious pioneer is viewing him from so immense a distance that he has hardly begun to see him at all. Christ was not a pioneer, but, if we must classify him, a prophetical messiah. And his place is not in something called religion, but in the Judaism of the first century. 'Religion' is a genus, like 'mammal'; and the genus as such does not exist, but only its species. We shall never meet a mere mammal coming up the road, but always a horse or a dog; and we shall never meet a simply religious man, but always a Christian or a Jew or a Huxleyite or an Evolutionary Semipantheist. The comparison of religious traditions is certainly of high interest, but it must be kept out of history itself, as damp must be kept out of timber. Christ must be seen in the crisis of early first-century Judaism, in which he lived, thought, preached and suffered. We may find insoluble the general problem, how a saintly man could encourage the acceptance of himself as the elect of God, in such a sense that all other men's divine election should be a by-product of his own. How this could be may be an insoluble problem, if we view it in general terms of what we are pleased to call religious psychology. But if we put religious psychology out of our heads, and enter the stream of Jewish spiritual existence as first-century records reveal it to us, then we may see the thing happening. 'Yes,' we may find ourselves saying, 'this is what Jesus does; it is intelligible in its place, it is historically inescapable.'

We may say, 'This is what Jesus does', but not, 'This is what he would obviously do.' For what Christ did was certainly not obvious, any more than what Socrates did when he provoked the court to condemn him was obvious, or what Plato did, when he so movingly dramatised Socrates's evidence, was obvious. Nothing that inspired minds do is obvious; but it is life, it convinces, it carries its evidence on its face, when it is seen in its historical place by a genuine historical discernment.

The higher the intensity of personal act, the more overpowering the constraint to recognise it as real. But the higher the intensity of personal act, the more complete the absurdity of listing it under any general heading. Those who think that to understand a thing is to exhibit it as the case of a rule, must be hard put to it by Shakespeare, Socrates, or St Paul, not to name Christ. You may indeed exhibit St Paul as the case of a rule; and by so doing you may give a good account of his Freudianness, but his Paulinity will have escaped you. His psychological type may indicate a type of attitude to womankind, but it was not a type of attitude to womankind which grasped the pen and shaped the words: 'I betrothed you to one man, that I might present you a chaste virgin to Christ.' The unique spirit of the Apostle wrote this, not a syndicate of psychological generalisations trading under the name of Operation Paul!

The historian is not concerned with the living individuality of single figures taken one by one and in isolation. How simple his task would be if he were! History does not deal with a staccato series of Robinson Crusoes, each living out his life in a human vacuum; it deals with a pattern of lives interacting upon one another. The point at which the pattern touches us, its would-be historians, is in the existences of our writing authorities. As a student of Christian origins I do not touch Christ, though as a Christian who receives the sacraments, I may. As a student, I touch Paul, Mark, and John. When I have learnt to know them, I may hope to perceive what in

them is reaction to Christ and to his saving acts; and so I may come
to perceive what manner of Christ it is, to whom they react.

I should have liked to pause, and to express regret and indignation at a manner of interpreting the evangelists which neglects, and
attempts to destroy, their living individuality. That St Paul is a
man, nobody doubts, nor that we have to understand him if we are
to understand the Christ who stands behind him. But when we turn
to St Mark, it is another matter: our oldest and best narrative authority is treated as individually negligible, a piecer together of traditions, a hack editor. We make haste to shoulder him out of the
way, that we may lay our hands upon an impersonal and disjointed
mass of tradition, which he is supposed to have had in his desk, or
in his memory. We pull the Marcan mosaic to bits, and then it is
amazing how free we find ourselves to reconstruct the ikon of Christ
according to enlightened principles, whether it be scientific probability or transcendental Neo-Calvinism that lies most near our
hearts.

But, you may say, it is no use pouring the vials of indignation
here. For it happens to be a fact that whereas we have abundant
data for reconstructing the personality of St Paul, for reconstructing
St Mark's we have virtually none. True, but irrelevant. For we are
not concerned to reconstruct St Mark as a missionary priest or a
husband and father, or as anything save the author of a gospel. The
only Mark we want is the Mark who became, for an unknown number of days and hours, the inspired act of meditating and writing
this book. We want nothing but his mental life, and of his mental
life no more than is enclosed between the first verse of his first
chapter and the eighth of his sixteenth. If this is a whole, living,
personal and continuous mental act, and I can touch it, then I can
touch a vital and significant part of that web of life which made up
the substance of Christian origins; and from it my thought can
spread to other and connected parts of the web, and ultimately the
centre, which is Christ himself. But if there is no important or profound or comprehensible mental life animating St Mark's book,
that is for the historian a heavy disappointment. Is St Mark a man
of straw? Then I have filled my arms with straw in laying hold of
him. And if I sit down, as the manner is, to pull the component
straws apart, and sort them into bundles, I shall reach no more than
arid botanical generalisations about the field from which they came,
the field that was sowed by the Sower who sows the word of God.

No efforts, then, can be too great to spend on the recovery of St Mark's mind, of a process of thought moving continuously through his book. If we cannot arrive at living by sympathy in his mental life, nothing can compensate us for our failure; and if we fail many times, it will still be better for us to try again, obstinately imputing our defeat to our own proved incomprehension, not to St Mark's supposed incoherence.

Our first historical task is to understand the men who give us the writings, and who, in the writings, give us themselves. But neither the men nor their writings can be understood in isolation. We cannot understand them unless we understand to what they are reacting. And that means, above all, that we must understand Christ. Put in general, like that, what I have just said sounds commonplace enough. Of course the aim of our New Testament history is to understand Christ; who disputes it? But what I want to say is something far more alarming. What I want to say is, that according to the canons of a sound historical procedure, we cannot establish what happened, we cannot establish the bare historical facts, without a personal understanding of Christ.

It would seem so much more comforting—it has seemed to many so much more comforting—to proceed by separate stages. First we will determine what the evangelists think and mean. When we have done that, we will compare their accounts, and check them by general probabilities and by our knowledge of the period; and so arrive at a decision of what were the facts of Christ's teaching and life. Having fixed the facts, we will take the third step, and advance to the interpretation of them. With humble diffidence we will conjecture what the mind of Christ may have been, if it expressed itself in words and actions such as these.

How comforting such a dividing-up of our work would be! We need not, in that case, imperil the historical facts by the terrible and thought-destroying task of understanding Christ, of moving in the mind which, according to our credal profession, made us and all the world, before it abased itself and stooped to pass the narrow door of Mary's womb. Into the abyss of that wisdom, into the heart of that devouring fire we need not plunge, until we have safely first established the historical facts. Vain evasion! Even if our faith permitted us to write a Christless history of Christ, the mere requirements of history-writing would not allow it. There is no establishing of the historic facts without an understanding of Christ.

We have not, to begin with, got the facts; we have only got second-hand reports of them. What we have to do is to find the causes which gave rise to these reports. How much was contributed by the devout theologising of the evangelist, how much by the credulity of the eye-witnesses, how much by the real action of Christ? It is obvious that these three factors cannot be estimated in independence of one another. If we could safely reduce the other two factors to zero, then we could confidently attribute the whole effect to the sole action of Christ, that is, we could simply believe the narratives about him as they stand. But we cannot confidently discount either the theologising evangelist or the credulous witness. Nor yet can we allow just so much for credulity and theology, subtract that, and attribute the remainder to Christ's naked action. No rules, forms, or principles of historical procedure can see us through such a task, or enable us to estimate the contributions of credulity and theological stylisation, independently of our estimate of what we can see Jesus of Nazareth to do.

Any example will suffice. Did Jesus ride into Jerusalem on an ass, with the circumstances of an arranged triumph? Well, Zechariah had prophesied that Sion's king should come to her riding on an ass. This being so, it is very possible that theological stylisation has exaggerated the chance ride of a footsore man into a messianic triumph, and that credulity has added the miraculous provision of a mount, the vision which saw an ass tethered on the further side of the hill, and the command which sent disciples to fetch it.

On the other hand, such preternatural vision is well evidenced in the lives of spiritual men; and Christ may have deliberately wished to fulfil Zechariah's oracle. But did he? Can we see him do it? Is it a proper part of his life and action, especially of his final invasion of Jerusalem. Only as we answer this question, shall we decide whether he sent for the ass and headed the triumph, or not.

There is no history of the things concerning Jesus (to use scriptural phrase) without an understanding of Jesus; any more than with any other biographical passage—it cannot be written without the understanding of the principal person concerned. Without understanding Jesus—but Jesus, what was Jesus? The secularist historians think they know; but their hypotheses produce no agreement, even among themselves, but wildly various travesties of what seems historical probability to Christians.

But we—how can we understand, for, as the Apostle says in

words borrowed from the prophet, Who has known the mind of the Lord, that he might be of his counsel? Understanding goes by sympathy: history is possible, because it studies men and the historian is a man himself. But Christ is not simply man, he is God-as-man, and mere natural human sympathy will not avail to know the mind of the Lord. If we lay down the dogma that Gospel history is just like any other history, we are committing ourselves to the proposition that Christ is just like any other man, or anyhow that his humanity is cut off from his deity and holds no communion with it. 'Who has known the mind of the Lord,' says St Paul, 'that he might be of his counsel?' But, as for us, he continues, we have the mind of Christ; and this, as he shows plainly in the context, is no natural sympathy with a human figure in his mere humanity, but a supernatural gift, by which we penetrate the abyss of wisdom, and move with the mind that moves the world.

The New Testament writings are perfectly clear, and perfectly realistic about this. This natural mind could not understand Jesus in his historical existence, not even the natural mind of his immediate companions. Nothing but the supernatural overflow of the mind of Jesus into them created that affinity whereby they could begin to understand him. Only God can understand God, even when God is incarnate. But God is in us by the Holy Ghost, and therefore we can know incarnate God. This is as true of us in our historical study, as it is of us at our prayers. We cannot know Christ in the history about him, except by the Holy Ghost. The historical understanding of Christ began in St Peter and the other recipients of the Pentecostal Gift. It continued in those who received both the historical testimony of St Peter's life and the gift of the Holy Ghost through the benediction of St Peter's hands. Later generations have received the historical testimony from the Church, the Church using the written scriptures as her norm of teaching; they have also received through the Church the Holy Ghost.

In one sense, then, Gospel history is just history, and its procedure is the same as any history's. It is the interpretation by sympathetic understanding of a web of interacting minds, with some of which, the evangelists, we are in immediate contact, with others, Christ and the Twelve, Caiaphas and Pilate, in a contact not in the same way immediate. So far Gospel history is like any other history. It is different, because one of the minds, Christ's, is not merely a natural mind, and can only be understood, therefore, by a super-

natural gift. There is therefore no neutral history of Christ common
to unbelievers and believers. We either accept, or do not accept, the
witness of the Holy Ghost. We understand the Christ who pro-
claimed himself the Son of God, because we understand, though but
partly, what it is for Christ to be the Son of God. And we understand what it is for Christ to be the Son of God, because we
perceive ourselves to be, in him, partakers of divinity. The God incarnate is not to us an unintelligible enigma, because our existence in
grace hangs upon the fringes of his incarnation. We know, on our
knees, and in the depth of our heart, what Christ is, by knowing
what he has made us: and we know what he has made us, by knowing
what he is.

ON THE SIN OF PRIDE

I Cor. i, 31. He that glorieth, let him glory in the Lord.

University Sermon, preached in St Mary's, Oxford, 1960

Your preacher is put up here by the long arm of a deceased but munificent benefactor, to denounce the sin of pride. The founder assumed, I take it, that in any foreseeable future the chosen spirits composing a University would be all too ready to get above themselves, and would need flattening down; a yearly application of pulpit rhetoric to the point would not be too frequent, even when supported by an annual commendation of humility—for, it must be supposed, in praising humility the orator would not be altogether able to conceal his disapprobation of pride.

There, then, is the text; and, if we let ourselves go on it, it would surely be an enjoyable theme. For just as the inveigher against luxury, in tearing down the Bower of Bliss, has occasion for succulent description of sensual delights, so the vocal enemy of pride may spread the glories of the peacock's tail, before he tramples on it.

How I wish I could promise you so colourful a sermon—but alas, I am unnerved by misgivings. For while pride is certainly a bad word in Christian ears, it is a valuable quality in manly bosoms. What young man will come to any good, who has not a touch of pride, and even a tincture of self-conceit? Humility may fill the Kingdom of Heaven; it will never populate a University. What brings men here, but a belief that they are better than the average— a belief sometimes upheld, and sometimes undermined, by the examiners in the schools. Even such a measure of confidence is too modest; it will be sad if entrants to our Colleges think no more of themselves, than that their general ability is above the average level. Let them entertain the secret conviction, that they have it in them to reveal new powers of nature, to compose masterpieces, to redirect the flow of taste, to evangelise unbelief, to prevent public ruin. Life will be hard with them; it will prune their high ambitions with a ruthless hand. But if there is nothing there to form, nothing will grow, or flower, or bear any fruit. Achievement is all rooted in the stock of pride. Nor is such pride unamiable; or rather, we pass a damning judgement on ourselves, if we find it so. What shall we say of the tutor, who prefers a docile humility in his pupils to the spirit which will make them uphold their arguments against his own? If they were reasonable beings, they would give in at once, for on any calculation, the expert will judge better than the layman and the veteran scholar know more than the novice. Only an irrational pride will sustain them in that valour of debate, which is, or should be, the joy of their teachers.

Well, but their conceit is neither amiable nor useful, if it blinds their eyes to the force of our reputations, and leads them to mis-judge the issue of the discussion. No, indeed, but it may be best of all if, admitting present defeat, they go away convinced that they have seen something out of the tail of the eye which they have not succeeded yet in bringing into focus; something which we have not seen, and of which they will convince us tomorrow. And here, per-haps, is the touchstone for discriminating what is good in pride, and what is evil. Innocent pride is positive, a glory in the use of talents, a promise of achievement. Bad pride is negative; it blinds us to truths of fact or even of reason, it disparages the achievements and hates the merits of others. And what can be worse? If thine eye be generous, thy whole person will be full of light; but if thine eye be grudging, thy whole person will be full of darkness: and if the light that is in thee be dark, how great is the darkness!

Our philosophical friends will point out to us the danger of founding a false paradox in a linguistic confusion. The Gospel de-nounces pride. Very well. Educators value pride. Very well. But is what the educator values the thing which the Gospel denounces? Perhaps, even, the difference between the two is a logical one. It is not that educators and preachers are speaking of different attitudes, under the one name. Perhaps the educators are speaking of an atti-tude, and the preachers of a vice. An attitude may be good, bad, or indifferent; a vice is bad by definition. Murder is never justifiable, though killing may be; and when pride is made the worst of capital sins, it means that province of villainy, which springs from the per-version of self-valuation. If pride is the name of a vice, it can never be the preacher's business to argue against it, but rather to make us hate it; or, may be, to unmask the hidden forms of it, when they might have got past in other clothes.

Here is a point on which a good deal of philosophy might well be expended by those who have the skill. We will go no further than to draw the simple moral that the admitted badness of the vice ought not to be made decisive for the value of the attitude. And with these words we will show philosophy the door.

Philosophy is no sooner out, than psychology knocks, and demands admission; for she, too, has much to say upon the subject: much about the deep roots which the pride-attitude strikes in the soil of our instinctive nature. A soul without an urge to self-assertion, or a concern for self-esteem, would be as much a monstrosity as a baby born without a right arm, or a left ear.

Shall we, then, pursue the question on psychological ground? An instructive pastoral lesson could certainly be learnt from a psychological examination of the way in which pride, or something like it, is inwoven with the very fibres of our minds. We should know better, from such a study, what sort of force we are wrestling with, when we meet pride in others, or in ourselves. Only we might be no clearer than before about the ultimate value to be placed in prideful attitudes of one or another sort. For insofar as psychology is an empirical science, it studies man as he is; that is to say, it studies a fallen creature; and it is always possible for conclusions psychologically established to be written off as nothing but the detailed pathology of original sin. So we will try to confirm the rights and define the limits of a proper pride, by a more general approach.

Pride is an irrational partiality; but then, so is affection. What is there in the girl who is loved, more than in any other girl? Nothing. A million others have equal graces, and are worthy of an equal appreciation; and God, who has an infinite heart, can find a place for whatever is lovely in any of his creatures. Our hearts are narrow and our sight is short. We think the world of the girl, or of the friend, because we cannot think the world of the world: that is a divine prerogative. The eyes of human partiality see more deeply than the eyes of human justice: we see in those to whom kinship, or sex, or sympathy unites us some little of the glory and the dearness, the richness and the vitality which God has scattered through the multitudes of mankind. If we were, like government clerks, condemned to equal justice; if we were forbidden to bestow on any claimant an attention we could not equally afford to all; how the life of the affections would be impoverished, and how shallow would be our acquaintance with the handiwork of God!

As with affection, so with pride. There is no more reason why we should exult or glory in the gifts and powers which God has given to us, than in those which he has given to any other of his creatures, if it is the worth of the things gloried in that is to be the test. But then, these are the treasures God has thrown into our very laps; and if we do not exult in these, in what shall we exult? Consider the pride of a mother in her first child. No woman ever can have brought forth such a creature. Goodness! he can say 'Mamma' and can stagger half way across the floor. She cannot help feeling such achievements to be unique: and yet, if she is a sensible woman, she can laugh at her own fatuity and recognise that the experience is common. When she meets the artless enthusiasm of other young mammas, she can find in it a bond of sympathy, not a subject of quarrel with her own. It is hard, in logic, to reconcile her assertion of her own maternal pride, with her acceptance of theirs; but this is where practical wisdom and verbal logic go apart. It would be a pity indeed if her sense of reason and justice stood in the way of her deep maternal exultation in her miraculous child; and no less a pity, if the logic of her personal pride made her disallow other women's.

It seems humiliating for even a part-time philosopher to confess, that the reasonable pursuit of human good involves the flouting of logic; but perhaps it will be some saving of face, if he helps himself out from the other field of his studies, and asserts that only the Divine Thinker himself can fully reconcile the rule of reason with the satisfaction of the heart. We can sometimes imitate the scope of the divine mind by diagrammatic and impartial surveys; and sometimes (at how great a remove!) approach the intensity of divine joy, or love, or exultation by sinking ourselves in partial objects. We cannot do both things at once, or even bring the two into a tolerable compromise. It is all very well to say that we ought so to phrase the language of pride, that it should imply no exclusive claims, and no disparagement of others; and so far as the public expression of pride is concerned, it is a sound social rule to impose upon our speech such limitations. But it is evident that the tactful utterances we allow ourselves towards our neighbours are incapable of doing justice to our own thoughts. I am proud of my family, though it was unmarked by any circumstances of outward distinction; proud of a tradition of family life in which the greatest tenderness was united with a Christian austerity; and it is useless to pretend that what I tell myself about my inheritance involves no assertion of singular privilege. It does. And it may be that it involves more; that it involves a negative arrogance, an actual disvaluing of other people's very different family roots. We have all of us to guard against such dangers. But if we look at those whom we should wish to imitate, we can see how such dangers are avoided. It is not by the logic of their lonely thoughts that these men break out of the closed circles of pride, but by the openness of their encounter with us, and their acceptance of our prides and enthusiasms in an equal sympathy.

Balaam, hired to curse Israel, went back on his bond, and, as Balak complained, did not curse them but blessed them altogether; and so it may seem that we have not cursed pride, as our duty was, but rather blessed it. Yet we would wish above all to persuade; and if we can help towards the discrimination between an innocent and a culpable pride, we have won our case with reasonable men. An indiscriminate onslaught on self-valuing attitudes might produce an immediate, but scarcely a lasting effect; today we are moved, but tomorrow, when the reasonable claims of a proper pride reassert themselves, we shall react against the unreality of an over-driven humility.

As against our neighbours, it will be enough if we allow them what we claim for ourselves. But such a degree of modesty is insufficient, when we face not our fellow creatures, but our common Creator. Pride is a matter of degree, in relation to our neighbours; in relation to our Maker it has no possible place. Pride is a tolerable, and even a laudable motive in a system of human morals; in religion it is nothing but sin, and indeed, typical of all sin.

Yet it is only too natural. For whereas pride in relation to our neighbours finds its check in the shock of our encounter with them, God is not so evidently encountered in this life; and the very pride which would be shattered by the vision of him is the reason why we fail to acknowledge him. Pride is a cause of blindness to our neighbours' merit: it is a cause of blindness to our creator's very existence, or anyhow, to his effective presence and his rightful sovereignty. What has happened? God displays his creative power chiefly in this, that he implants in his creatures an almost limitless energy of existence, and self-developing force. The very elements of nature exercise a boundless self-expression with which the mind of an atomic age is all too painfully acquainted. It is as though every sort of natural being were set to absolutise itself, and to be the whole universe if it can. Admittedly it cannot: its rivals check it. And it is out of this rivalry of physical self-assertions that God has been pleased to make the world. On the conscious and rational level, the creatures of God exult in a Godlike power, and fret against any limits set to the exercise of it. If we encounter God, we must recognise the very origin and institutor of our creative aspirations; but if we seem not to encounter him, but merely a feigned tale of a divine authority, we rebel against it in the name of the divine image we bear. To be converted is to repent our pride in dust and ashes, to see that we have so gloried in imported powers, as to deny and violate the majesty of glory itself. And after our conversion, we have constantly to acknowledge in ourselves and to wonder at the arrogance, which dares still to live by the choice of its own will, and so seldom even to consider the good pleasure of a compassionate and self-revealing God.

The accusation is brought by the Christian against himself: not, let us hope, against his unbelieving neighbour. For while it is true that unbelief is largely based on pride, it is a pride of which the unbeliever is not personally guilty. It is original sin, a godless attitude in which he has been reared, and out of which he has never been able to break; not actual sin, an attitude which, when there was a better alternative before him, he wilfully preferred to embrace. The pride of unbelievers, which cuts them off from the fountain of living waters is surely the object of divine compassion alone. The pride of Christians, who revolt from a revealed and sovereign love, is the true object of indignation: an indignation which would destroy us, were it not that mercy turns it to a cleansing fire: and in burning our vanity away, preserves in us that heavenly substance which our redemption has planted in us, the life of Jesus Christ our Lord.

2.

For Faith

WHAT IS GOD?

In my hot-headed youth, I thought I would bring about a reformation of the language. Among other refinements I hoped to introduce was the general substitution of 'relative' for 'relation' when referring to one's sisters, cousins or aunts. How could a cousin *be* a relation? I stand in a relation to him, and in virtue of that relation he is relative to me. But 'my relations'—how did so preposterous a usage come about? I suppose it began like this. On hearing Mr X casually remark that he was great-nephew to the Marquis of Bute, 'Sir,' you exclaimed, 'that is a highly respectable relation'—relation, that is, in which to stand. But next day, with that grammatical carelessness which is all too common, you found yourself alluding to 'X's highly respectable relation, the Marquis of Bute'. And so a concrete nobleman came to be defined as a mere abstraction of relatedness to a great-nephew, as though he derived his whole being and function from connection with that unnecessary young man: a very unreasonable description; for so far from exercising the existence of a great-uncle, the noble marquis might be only indistinctly aware of his great-nephew's ever having been born.

To define others by relation to ourselves is a sublime, if unconscious, egotism. It may not matter all that in human affairs, but when it is carried into theology it causes trouble. God is my Father. His fatherhood to me is indeed a relation, for it constitutes me as the child of God. But it is not a relation which defines for me what God is. If I begin my theology with the thought of 'a supernatural father for me', I quickly arrive at the much-derided picture of a manlike majesty somewhere up there in the sky. Rational belief in God the Father Almighty has nothing to do with such childishness. God— ah, he is God; how dare I try to say what God is? And *yet* he is my Father, for he has called me into being, and given me just so much kinship to himself, that I can name his name and choose—if only I do choose—his holy will. But in himself, what is he?

Is it right even to ask the question? We are told in a very old and

55

doubtless very barbarous tale how Jacob wrestled with God in the dark, and tried to make him declare what he was; but as dawn broke God put a wrestler's touch on Jacob, which disabled him while the invisible slipped from his grasp. God had not revealed what he was, but he had told Jacob what Jacob was, and had blessed him. And so it is practical doctrine that if we wrestle with God's holy will we shall find out what we are, and what we are called to be; we shall not find out what God is, for all the assurance we gain that his will indeed wrestled with ours, and that we have his blessing.

The doctrine is good; and it is certain folly to think one will ever say what God is. One must say something, though, however foolish it sounds in the ears of heaven. For we must think something when we think of God, never mind how short we fall of the mark at which our thoughts are aimed. So now let me commit this great folly, and say what is God.

Shall I say he is the prime cause and maker of all things? I shall not err; only I shall still have defined him by a relation, in that all things are *from* him. I shall not have said what is he. But I do see that all things that are made have a hallmark on them, the sign of their createdness; the sign being this, that they are all limited expressions of what a thing can be; any one of them might just as well have been a good deal otherwise; each of them has been shut up to being no more than what it is. Say if you will that each thing and each fact is determined to be what it is by its place in the total universe. Very well; but even this whole great baffling universe of stars is itself just one scatter and spread of material stuff, one arrangement among all the arrangements there might have been. To believe in God is to believe that the ultimate reason why things are so and not otherwise, is that he has willed them to be so. What then is he? God is will, and he is will subject to no such limitations as he has measured out to his creatures. His is the being which knows no barriers; he always is all that he wills to be, and wills to be all that he is.

What have I said? Have I committed the notorious folly of saying what is God? I have not; for I have not pretended to state what sort of a life it must be, that has the scope my words have just attributed to the life and action of God. Let me take a feeble though obvious comparison. There was a time I can just remember when I knew that people wrote, received and read letters, and made themselves understood by that channel; but I had no notion of the principle of the thing, of how words could be scripted, or script convey words. I scribbled with a pencil, and spoilt much paper in my play. Though I wrote nothing, I thought I was writing, for I did not know what writing was. I knew that my elders sent speech through scribbled lines; how they did it, I did not know. And so with my adult knowledge of the life of God; I know that it is a life and action such as to suffer no limits, to be subject to no charter of existence, to be simply sovereign and free. But what must the divine life be, to achieve all this? I do not know.

I do not know; only I find in myself this clue, this vestige of divinity, that my thought climbs out of my skin, and attempts an impartial survey of the universe, with my own body in it: that my will battles against the limitations of character of circumstance, and attempts a sovereign mastery. And so I can at least frame the question, what would that mind be, that saw all things in the very truth of their being, without disguise; what would that will be, which achieved its whole aspiration without impediment? I can ask the question, I cannot answer it. For the answer is what God is; and that is what I am not.

Enough, then, of this folly. We have looked into the abyss just far enough to remind ourselves of the infinite deep. And that is God. The Catholic Faith in God the Father Almighty is not the belief that we have a relation in heaven, a Father of much dignity and power. It is a faith really consisting of two parts, to be kept distinct and not to be confused. First, the supreme being, cause and good is Almighty God, infinite Spirit. Second, this God is Father, for he has chosen to give himself children.

I don't know whether any of you need to be warned against the more stultifying forms of textbook orthodoxy—because there is a way of so stating the doctrine of the Trinity as to deny that God simply is the Father Almighty, on the ground that God is every person of the Trinity equally. But that is to put the matter badly. God is God, and there is no God but he. He is eternally the Father because he has never willed to be alone; and so it has never been that he has not given himself a Son on whom he everlastingly bestows all that he himself either has or is; the Son of God being so truly God's Son, as to lack nothing his Father possesses. It remains nevertheless that the Father is not only Father to his Son, he is also God to him. His Father's giving him all he has does not make him worship his Father the less. How should it? Why do we men worship God? Because he has given us so little, or because he has given us so much? In worshipping God, we worship a bottomless bounty. We cannot return him a limitless worship, limited as we are. His infinite Son gives him infinite thanks for an infinite gift; and when he appears among us men, for our salvation, he comes as our fellow-worshipper; his Father is ours, his God is ours.

I have called it a sort of folly to say what the divine life is. It's a folly, if so, that we can easily renounce; for to have a practical knowledge of God we need not penetrate the heart of mystery or find the top of being. We cannot ascend unto his height, but why should we attempt it? He comes down into our valley. How foolish was Nimrod, who thought by the hands of ten thousand slaves to rear at Babel a tower reaching the gods! And how blessed was Abraham, when God came to him in the guise of a travelling man, and ate at his table, and called him his friend! In the old tale it is by a special disguise that God comes to the patriarch; but that is poetry. For God identifies himself unrestrictedly with every one of his creatures, he thinks and knows them from within, his creative thought is expressed in their very being; for else, how should they exist? His whole work of creation is a coming down from heaven, an indwelling of his creatures; his heart goes with them, he looks at us out of their eyes. Above all, God becomes human in men; he is met in our neighbour, he speaks in the depth of our heart; not because the heart of our heart is other than we, but because it is our very self, the self God makes, wills and directs. The Son of God came to reconcile us with God in reconciling us with the truth of ourselves; and he it is that leads, that studies, that inflames our adoration of his God and ours, his Father and our Father; to whom through that most blessed Son, by inspiration of the Holy Ghost, be ascribed as is most justly due all might, dominion, majesty and power, henceforth and for ever.

HOW CAN WE BE SURE OF GOD?

—preached in the Cowley Fathers' Church, Oxford, 1967

There is something absurd, or almost indecent, in the task I have been given this morning. We are here before God's altar, pledging our souls to him: we are considering what his holy will lays upon us, to make our self-oblation an actuality; we are to receive at his appointment the body and blood of his incarnate Son under a mystery of bread and wine; we are to give thanks to him for infinite and inexpressible acts of mercy in our creation and in our redemption. And now in the midst of this we are to pause, and ask ourselves how we can be sure of God at all. What is our predicament like? I will tell you what it is like. Yesterday I had to replace a lamp at a height of fourteen feet in the clear middle of the ceiling: and my stepladder wouldn't reach. For the first time I found a practical use for the bound volumes of the *University Gazette* bequeathed me by my predecessors in office; and balancing a pile of them on top of the steps, I reared myself gingerly up. I had just unscrewed the globe when I asked myself whether I was securely placed. No sooner the question asked, than I trembled at the knees, and came near to losing my balance by thinking of it. Pull yourself together, I said, get on with the job, that way safety lies—and so I did; and so I remain in one piece, to come and address you this morning. I hardly need to draw the moral of the comparison. It is not in looking at our faith that we have conviction of God, but in looking at God, and in obeying him. God can convince us of God, nothing else and no one else can: attend the Mass well, make a good communion, pray for the grace you need, and you will know that you are not dealing with the empty air.

Think of my mother, now—you have known women like her, though few, perhaps, as good—a more unphilosophical thinker it would be difficult to find. Now suppose that in the heyday of my adolescent intellectualism I had told her that she had no right to her fervent evangelical faith, not being able to put together half a dozen consistent sentences in justification of her mere belief in God.

What would she had said? She would have told me that admired
intellects had bothered themselves with such enquiries, and been
able to satisfy their minds: for her part, God had given her faith,
and God had never let her down except it was by her manifest fault.

Well, but surely the Warden of Keble isn't going to preach you
sheer anti-intellectualism—no, he isn't: you are perfectly right. The
centre of your Christian conviction, whatever you may think, will be
where my mother's was—in your exploration of grace, in your walking with God. But faith perishes if it is walled in, or confined. If it
is anywhere, it must be everywhere, like God himself: if God is in
your life, he is in all things, for he is God. You must be able to
spread the area of your recognition for him, and the basis of your
conviction about him, as widely as your thought will range.

And now today, on Septuagesima, we think of God's illimitable
creation; so let me say something about that. Can I honestly claim
to see this mighty spread of galaxies as God's handiwork—as need-
ing him for their existence? I think it is best here to be very modest
in one's assertions. I will even begin by something with which a
candid atheist ought to agree. It is this: the world raises a question
which the world doesn't answer: you can't find within the world an
explanation why the world's the way it is. All explanations come
back to the laws of Nature: but we can't account for the laws. We
must say they are what they are, and there it is. Again, all explanations of a present state of affairs carry us back to a previous state of
affairs; we never come to a state of affairs which explains itself, or
has to be the way it is. Why are Nature's laws as they are? And why
are brute facts the way they are? There is no answer within the
world.

I say that a candid atheist should agree with us. But only up to a
point—he will say that the question the world raises and the world
doesn't answer is an empty and fantastic question, since it admits
of no answer, and we can do nothing with it: it is like those silly
questions little children go on asking beyond all meaning and all
sense: Mummy, why is that a dog? Don't be silly, darling, a dog
is a dog.

So the atheist thinks, poor man, because he is an atheist. Not that
we are to pretend that we believers can get behind the scenes of
Nature, and see God making things be the way they are. Of course
we can't. Indeed, if we *could* press behind the scenes of Nature,
there'd be nothing for us to see. God acts by simple will; and we

cannot see the will of God except in what that will has created. There is only one point at which we can possibly touch the nerve of God's creative action, or experience creation taking place: and that is in our own life. The believer draws his active Christian existence out of the wellspring of divine creation, he prays prayers which become the very act of God's will in his will. Because we have God under the root of our being we cannot help but acknowledge him at the root of all the world's being. So it is that, where the atheist sees the search for an ultimate explanation of things as a meaningless 'Why', we see it as the searching out of God's creative power.

I will tell you how to disbelieve in God. Split the evidence up, and keep it apart. Keep the mystery of the world's origin carefully separate from your experience of God, and then you can say that the cosmic facts are dumb: they raise a question, they give no answer. Keep the believer's experience of God by itself, and away from the general mystery of nature; then you can say that it's so peculiar, so odd a little fact in this vast indifferent universe, that to attach universal importance to it is too absurd. Then on the other side, be careful to keep the barriers up between the God in you and the God in Christ. Then you can say of your own Christianity (as you must indeed confess) that it's too slight a thing to support the towering edifice of faith. Meanwhile, shutting Christ off in a separate compartment of your mind, you can say that the idea of a God-Man is a mere erratic streak, with nothing to support it in the whole range of experience.

I have told you how to disbelieve. Now I will tell you how to believe. Just do the opposite: pull all these mental barriers down. Where can I be sure of God? In Christ, yes, of course, in Christ: if Christ was not the breakthrough of God showing his hand in a part of the world, where are we to look for it? But is not God-in-man too great a stretch of miracle to be believed? No indeed, for God-in-man overflows from Christ and shows many shining tokens in the saints; and even the clue to what it is, it reveals in our own poor lives. Poor they are, and too thin to bear the weight of evidence: but then they do not stand alone. We see clearly enough that what we have an inkling of, the saints apprehend, and Christ simply achieves. Ah, but is not this whole phenomenon of life invaded by the divine a mere freak in the vast material solid of the universe? Nonsense, the universe isn't solid at all: it is, as a totality, unexplained and subject to the appointment of creative will in all its infinite detail.

We believe in One God, One not only in the unity of his substance but in the unbroken wholeness of his action. All the work of God is one mighty doing from the beginning to the end, and can only be seen in its mind-convincing force when it is so taken. It is One God who calls being out of nothing, and Jesus from a virgin womb, and life from the dead; who revives our languid souls by penitence, and promises to sinful men redeemed the vision of his face, in Jesus Christ our Lord.

THE PAINTER'S COLOURS

—preached in Christ Church Cathedral, Oxford, 1963

It seems as though we were in for a year of electioneering. It is a discouraging prospect, isn't it? Electioneering is so awful. Everything has to be discussed at a level of grotesque simplification; rational debate becomes impossible. It is often little better in public exchanges between Christians and their critics. I read in the press how a scientific professor exclaims that scientists know more about God's creation than Bishops and Church leaders do. To which an Archbishop retorts, the man is talking nonsense; God's creation involves sacrifice and scientists know nothing about sacrifice. I dare say both speakers are misreported, but taking the exchange as it stands, what can a philosopher do but weep? The professor's remark is, to start with, hopelessly ambiguous. Distinguish the senses, and there's nothing left to discuss; for in one sense his dictum is self-evidently true, in another as evidently false. Who knows about *God's creation*? If by God's creation you mean the physical system God has instituted, then the scientist has a sort of knowledge about it to which no one else, and least of all a bishop, pretends. But if by God's creation you mean 'what the Creator's will intends and achieves', then that is not a subject on which a scientist has a syllable to say. In one sense, the supplier of artists' materials knows what paintings are, for they are certainly unquestionably paints and canvas. In another sense, he knows nothing about it. The painter knows, for he understands the game which is played with these substances.

Well, but if we are to apply the analogy to creation, God both supplies the materials and paints the picture: he is the expert, then, in both fields. Yes, of course, and that goes without saying: God is the universal expert. The most any human experts can do is to think some of God's thoughts after him. The scientist obtains insight into the structure of the materials, by direct examination; but when it comes to understanding, or appreciating the picture God paints, then where are we? If we were utterly incapable of aesthetic

63

appreciation, we could never know anything about a painted picture; if we have some inklings, then perhaps we are in a position to comprehend, if the painter himself will explain himself to us.

Now admittedly human artists are often ludicrously bad at explaining themselves. Their genius is in their finger-tips. They create by a sort of inspiration or possession, as though a power not themselves employed them; they know not what they do. But no such limitation of knowledge applies to God. He knows what it is that he does, and in this he differs most startlingly from us men and all along the line. Jesus said that his executioners knew not what they did, an ignorance which gave them a hope of divine forgiveness. And we are all in the same position, all the time. The only acts which we fully understand and master are trivial acts. If I am playing a game of noughts and crosses against a child, I know exactly what I am doing in placing my mark, for there is no great mystery about the principles of that game. But if I intervene in a discussion on the Governing Body of my College, then heaven knows what I am up to, and my colleague's guesses at my game are very likely as good as my own.

But God's work is completely perspicuous to him; he does what he means, and means what he does: and so, if he pleases to explain his mind to us, he can.

Scientific professors are perfectly within their rights, if they resent theologians giving themselves airs. Theologians have no claim whatever to be pleased with themselves, for, unlike the scientist, the theologian makes no discoveries: he merely interprets and relays the self-disclosure of God. A scientist may be a creative genius: not so a theologian.

So God paints the picture, and God explains the effect at which he aims; he opens our eyes to it. Such is our parable; like all parables, it illuminates, and like all parables, it is liable to mislead. For if we say 'the world is the masterpiece of the divine painter' we make a grotesquely false suggestion. The painter creates *a* picture; it is as a unit that it has its pictorial being and value. It exists as an arrangement for being looked at. But God does not create *a* world. Admittedly the world offers an arrangement to be looked at, always supposing that any mind is capable of getting it all into focus. Perhaps the seven archangels can manage it: or perhaps only the four cherubim can pull it off. But however that may be, the world's function is not to be a painted show, for men, or for angels, or for cherubim, or for the all-seeing God himself to contemplate. The world's function is to exist and to act with inexhaustible energy, imitating in endless variety the riches of God's own absolute vitality. And this the world does not do as a whole, but only in its constituent parts. To say that the world exists, is like saying that a swarm of bees exists. The swarm only exists, because each of the bees exists, and because they all cling together. We are all aware of the dangerous fallacies which arise through the personification or hypostatisation of collectives. There is no Uncle Sam, no Britannia or John Bull, and when Adolf Hitler claimed to impersonate the German Soul, there was no need to pay him any extra attention on that ground. But the most staggering of all hypostatised collectives is the world. If I say, that there's no such thing as the world, don't think I've joined the Christian Scientists. There's no such *thing* as the world, but all the things in the world exist: and, existing, they make up the world. For God has not only made all the things in the world, he has made them to make up a world: and that's his masterpiece.

Now when we claim that God, the sole supreme artist, has revealed to us the drift and the intention of his work, we are talking about God as the creator of each single creature, and not about God as the cosmic designer. As to cosmic design, we may fairly concede to the astronomers and physicists that they know all that is so far known about it: theology has not a syllable to add. Creation, as a revealed truth, is concerned with the existence of single creatures. Now we cannot taste or appreciate creaturely existence except in ourselves, and in others like us. In our friends—why, yes, if we love them as ourselves. In our enemies, oh, far less clearly; for dislike shutters our eyes. In brute beasts, perhaps, dogs, cats, and horses: but ants, bees, slugs and snails—what do you think? I would say, No.

So then, in this range of thinking, human existence is our sample of existence. Taught to appreciate our own being as created, we attribute createdness to a million other things; for we see that they are no more sufficient to exist of themselves than we are.

There is no scandal or absurdity, then, in admitting that the Christian doctrine of creation is centred upon the two-legged creature, man. Our faith teaches us to taste the quality and the drift of our own dependence upon God; perceiving that we exist by his good pleasure, we cannot but know that everything else does, also.

We can perhaps see now that it is not altogether surprising if

5

unbelievers fail to feel the force of arguments in proof of a creator. The arguments can be stated, but they cannot compel belief, as a proof in mathematics can compel belief. Speaking broadly, we can say that men will not admit a creator unless they are willing and able to live out their own createdness in a day-to-day dependence upon God.

I have been saying all along that creation is a doctrine which the Creator himself reveals: the painter discloses to us the nature of his work. You may fairly ask me, how and where does God make such a revelation? Do you really mean to tell us that because an old Jewish writer threw together a pile of age-old myths in the book called Genesis, we are assured of the very mind and speech of God? No, I mean no such thing. The centre and the seal of revelation is Jesus Christ alone. The significance of Genesis is, that it contains the picture of an idea which Christ proved by living it out. For it is not simply that Jesus saw the handiwork of God in lilies, and his providence in the fall of a sparrow. It is that he wagered his life on creative power. Who can raise the dead? No one: in the literal sense, not God himself. The dead are not raised: immortalised men are not galvanised corpses. What is called the resurrection of the dead is a remaking of their life, in a stuff and in a fashion which are known to God alone. If we are made, we can be remade: he who created can create anew. Jesus Christ experimented with creation when he threw himself and all the world's hopes into nothingness, by the death of the cross.

We shall not deeply and honestly believe that the Painter paints the picture until we are willing to be liquid colours under his brush; and how little do we even pray for that, let alone live it! But that is what heaven will be; a life in which the very countenance of God is constantly and visibly portrayed in the changing colours of his creatures' lives. Creation, like everything else, will be perfectly manifest for the first time in heaven. For there, the blessed by their whole existence set forth the manifold mastery of God: and by their lives as well as with their lips ascribe as is most justly due to God the Father, Son and Holy Ghost, one deity in three persons, all might, dominion, majesty and praise, through ages everlasting.

WHAT IS FAITH IN GOD?

—preached in St Mary's, Oxford, 1960

'Come in, my dear man, come in!' The voices sounded quite every-day and quite full-blooded. But I suppose I must have been dreaming, for the scene was nothing earthly. I was being welcomed into the next world. But by whom? Who were these vaguely familiar presences? Could they be—yes, they were—a collection of those scholars who in several ages, had written expositions of St John's Revelation. 'So you wrote one too', they said to me as they took me by the hand. I blushingly admitted it. 'In that case,' they said, 'you will find a great deal to surprise you here.' I began to look round, but before I could adjust my eyes to the brightness of the light, I awoke.

And no doubt everything we think now about that great mystery will seem childish and absurd when we see face to face. However long and venerable our beards may grow in this world, we remain silly little people in the eyes of the blessed. Nevertheless there are degrees of immaturity, even in this infancy of the soul; one does grow out of some things between one's teens and one's fifties; and among them is a worry about the nature of the act of faith. How can I believe? How does one do it? we used to ask ourselves, as though it were a matter of learning a set of dancing steps or of mastering a method in algebra. But of course the first point about believing is, that if you make yourself do it, you aren't believing, you are only pretending. To believe is to accept the force of the evidence. The recipe for believing is just to get the object into focus, and to attend steadily to it. That may not be easy: there are many distractions: and (alas!) many strong motives for shutting one's eyes. St Augustine would have admitted the force of the Gospel evidence many months before he did, if it hadn't meant putting away his mistress. There was much call for effort here; but not for an effort to comprehend the nature of the act of faith. The less belief is thought about, the better it functions; one can apply here Hilaire Belloc's lesson for the young.

The water beetle here shall teach
A lesson far beyond your reach;
He flabbergasts the human race
By gliding on the water's face
With ease, celerity and grace!
But if he ever paused to think
Of how he did it, he would sink.

All the water beetle needs to know is that there is something over there worth going for; nature does the rest. So St Peter, when he walked on the water to go to our Lord. His troubles began when he started to think what an astonishing and dangerous thing it was, to be balancing his steps on the storm-lashed waves.

The moral of course is general. It is not special to faith. Speculations on the nature of love do not help us to love one another; all that is wanted is attention to our fellow-being, and the removal of obstacles, such as restlessness, prejudice, selfishness and fear.

That sounds very well, you may say: but it doesn't fit the facts. What is the use of saying that belief in God will follow from attention to realities, and candour in the mind? For were this all, the attentive and candid would be found to be believers; and the more so, in proportion as their mental powers were the greater. But we find that our experts in mental attentiveness, and in dispassionate candour, are often agnostics, for example, our most distinguished philosophers. This is really a weighty objection which no thoughtful man can fail to appreciate. What shall we say to it? We must say that attentiveness and candour in different fields of observation can be very different qualities, or anyhow, that they may belong to different men. A man who is attentive to logical form, or to scientific facts, and candid in assessing the force and bearing of what he studies, may be superficial, hasty and prejudiced in his appreciation of personal situations.

If you will put up with my being a bit more donnish, and all too like some people whom I think I am about to criticise, I will make a few remarks here about the history of a word. The Bible praises wisdom both as a gift of God, and as a gift by which men come to know God. The servants of God, thoughtful Israelites, or, later, Christians were the true lovers of wisdom, philo-sophoi or philosophers: were, in reality, what the Greek sages claimed to be. And what was this wisdom which Greeks sought, and which God's people possessed? I should say that, both to Greeks and Israelites, wisdom consisted of two things: knowing how to live, in the most profound and human sense—how to make of your life what your life was made for: that was the one part of wisdom. And the other was inseparable from it: to know those truths about yourself, and about the realities surrounding you, which you must know if you are to respond appropriately to the demands of your situation, and so live truly well. This was wisdom: and so the philosophers or lovers of wisdom studied to know the world in those aspects of it which determine the good for man, and to know the true direction and pattern of that human good.

It was of course the constant criticism levelled against the old philosophers that they were not saints or sages, but logical pedants. The criticism might be disputed as unjust—Socrates at least was genuinely wise—but it was never set aside as irrelevant: no one said, 'Oh, but philosophy has nothing to do with a saintly wisdom: it is a technical craft of logical analysis. There is no more reason why philosophers should be wise, than why any other sort of man should be so: the butchers, bakers or candlestick makers.' In that ancient world no one would have dreamt of saying this sort of thing. But this is exactly what now of course would be said. It is plain, then, that philosophy has changed its meaning: a philosopher is no longer supposed to be a wise man.

Well, I do not wish to reconstruct the old Greek idol; history has smashed it; we may as well concede that the Greek programme for becoming wise was fundamentally misdirected, and that the only solid fruit it has borne has been the development of linguistic theory. But if we have ceased to expect our philosophers to be wise, need we trouble our heads greatly about their tendencies to believe or not to believe in God? We said that attentiveness and candour were the conditions of belief; but when it is religious belief that is in question, the attentiveness and the candour need to be exercised in the field of wisdom, if they are to bear upon the point. It would be odious to quote names, but some of our most renowned philosophers have seemed most unwise: have proved unable to manage their matrimonial affairs with happiness or even with tolerable dignity; or to handle their growing children with any marked success. Worse than that: they have sometimes seemed to be men of paper, for whom the universe is reduced to written propositions. I do not wish to attack an art or a science (whichever it is) on which

I have spent a good part of my life; it is an instrument of clarification most useful in many fields and not least in theology, where it is indeed most needed. But like all specialisms it is apt to take toll of the humanity of those who devote themselves to it. There are philosophers who are genuine sages, but I do not think that they are many.

Well, though broadcasting and television have given the philosophers a new notoriety, they still are not the arbiters of modern thought. Whether the philosophical ingredient is large or small, there is such a thing as modern mindedness, and what we ought to be considering is what it can mean for modern man to believe in God. Is that what we ought to be considering? No, I don't think it is. The question is preposterous, in the literal sense of the term, that is, like a sweater too hastily pulled on; you have got it back to front. You might as well suppose the unfortunate bitch who went up in the sputnik, to have occupied her tedious solitude with the question, what is it like for a space traveller to be a four-footed beast? An absurd approach, obviously; she is, and always was, a four-footed beast, being of the canine kind. What she can fairly consider is, what it is like for a four-footed beast such as she is, to be whizzing through space in a rocket, instead of enjoying those terrestrial conditions for which the mammalian species appear to be designed. Our God-relatedness, our groundedness in God, is the most permanent aspect of our being: why, it was there in the predestining intention of God before we were either born or thought of; and it remains in eternity, when all this universe shall have dissolved. We cannot sensibly ask, what it is like for a creature who is being rocketed through the twentieth century to be grounded in God, and to know that fact: what we can ask is, what it is like for a creature drawing his life from God, to be rocketed through the twentieth century.

That is not to deny, that the expression of our faith in God will take special forms in this age, forms practical as well as verbal: and no doubt a great deal can be said about these forms of action and of statement. Nevertheless, to believe in God in the second half of the twentieth century is fundamentally just to believe in God, just as to be born or to die in the twentieth century is, fundamentally, to be born and to die: however much midwifery eases the birth or morphia disguises the death.

A modern believer in God, like any other believer in God, can say like this: special sciences give me many useful and interesting diagrams of the way things act; even to the furthest confines of astronomical space. But the only example in which I can feel the nerve of existence, or the quality of life, is in myself, and in those who so resemble me; that myself gives me a clue to what they also are. Whether I like it or not, I must accept man as my specimen creature, and judge of other existences by whatever analogy they bear to my own. Now I believe in God: that is, I receive this being of mine as a gift, a blessing, and a duty, owed to a supreme and perfect will, a will which shines through the action of my nature, and the circumstances of my lot: a will which can be attended to, and acknowledged in prayer and obedience. And if my own life comes to me as an obligation, a blessing, and a gift, how much more the lives and persons of my neighbours and friends, in whom the divine creativity is so multiplied, and set in front of me before my very eyes! In them God has given me my natural happiness; they are so much more the objects of love and delight to me than I can be to myself. Nothing can obscure the God in them, but my own wilful sin; and even that drives me to seek the living mercy of the Godhead, in whom friendship and society have their perfection through the love of the Father and the Son, which is the Holy Ghost: to whom therefore God in three Persons, be ascribed as is most justly due, all might, dominion, majesty and power, henceforth and forever.

WHAT IS FAITH IN GOD?

say that special success gives one many useful and interesting
diagrams of the way things are seen in the further reaches of
astronomical space. But that just exemplifies in which I am... for the
nerve of each...
who so examine may that myself given... that to what I may also...
creature, and...of value, or whatever analogy they
bear to my own. Now I believe in God, that is, I believe this being...

THINKING THE TRINITY

—preached in Trinity College Chapel, Oxford, on Trinity Sunday, 1961

When we were in America—and it feels odd, I must say, being in
America. They treat the academic visitor as a talking book; the text
is something you published twenty years ago, but footnotes, they
hope are going to spurt *viva voce* from your living person, wherever
they stick a pin into you. Under this sort of treatment, you can see
that it is difficult not to grow a trifle pompous. And so there we
were in a corner of New York, holding an open forum (or was it a
colloquium?) and laying down the law about the action of the divine
providence in the balancing of goods and evils. Some discussion
ensued; until a Jewish scholar, whose presence had been hitherto
unnoticed, pricked our little bubble for us. Not that he broke in—
he waited for a full pause in the conversation; and when he spoke,
it was with much gentleness. He had one of those thoughtful
Jewish faces that seem to be moulded by a sense of their people's
suffering, but at the same time by a patient faith in the God of
Israel. He found it surprising, he said, to hear Christian theologians
speculate so confidently on the place of pain and disaster in the
counsels of God—a mystery which, not unnaturally, had occupied
the Jewish mind a good deal. He said that he would express his own
sense of the matter in a Jewish form, by quoting a rabbi of older days.

The rabbi's pupils came one morning and sat before him. They
asked him the providential reason of some natural evil that had
befallen—let us say that it was a neighbour's premature death. 'My
children,' said the rabbi, 'there are questions into which a man may
enter, and there is no way back out of them. Again, there are questions a man may enter upon, and there is a way back. And it is the
first part of wisdom, when any question is proposed, to decide of
which sort it is. Now I tell you that the question, why God permits
this or that natural evil, is among the questions allowing of no way
back, nor of any answer. And why? I will tell you this also. The
Holy One (Blessed be He!) filled all immensity before the world
was, and there was no place where He was not; and so neither was

72

there any place where a world could be; for He was all, and in all.
What did He do? He drew back the skirts of His glory, to make a
little space where He was not; and there He created the world.
And so, where the world is, there He is not. And that is why we
look in vain for His hand in the chances of nature. Nevertheless
(Blessed be He!) He has visited us with His lovingkindness.'

So said our Jewish philosopher; and when he had spoken, we had
little appetite for resuming our previous discussion. We wanted to
ponder the words of his ancient sage. There seemed to be a deep
sense in them, but not a sense that lay on the surface. Obviously it
takes you nowhere, to speak of God's being present or absent, in
any plain way, at one place or another. In one way, he is everywhere absent, for no place bodily contains Him. In another way, he
is everywhere present; since whatever exists manifests His present
will that it should exist; and as the Psalmist says, 'If I go down into
hell, thou art there also.' For hell would not be, if God's will for its
existence were withdrawn from it.

What, then, had the rabbi meant, when he spoke of God's vacat-
ing a space to allow for a world? We asked our Jewish friend, and
he said the meaning was this: God gave the world room to be itself.
He would not so inhabit it as to make it the passive reflection of His
own ideas; or like the machine which does no more than embody
the design of its constructor, and perform the wishes of its manipu-
lator. God made the world, but He did not just make it; He made it
make itself; for only so could it be itself. He released a half chaos of
brimless forces as alien from His own being as anything could well
be; and they blinded away, not in the paths of a godlike wisdom, but
according to the very limited principles of action implanted in each.
Nevertheless (said the rabbi), the Holy One has visited us with His
lovingkindness; by an invisible art, and by a secret attraction, he
has brought out of a blind interplay of forces many organised
intricacies and much sentient life.

What, then, is the moral of the fable? The world is not like God,
though it reveals His power and His glory. Nature is infinitely
wasteful, but God wastes nothing. She is unfeeling; he is compassionate. She is blind; he is wise. For at the beginning and
bottom of nature, there is a withdrawal, we may almost say a self-
banishment, of God. Nature is not divine; we cannot be nature-
worshippers, except by projecting upon nature a gilded image of
our dreams. God made the world in unlikeness to himself; we look

there in vain for the lineaments of his face. He made man in his own similitude, and it is in the face of man that we must look for the countenance of God.

Or rather, not in the face of man, but in the faces of men, turned towards one another; the light of understanding that passes between their eyes, in a sense that sounds through the interchange of their speech, in mutual liking kindled from heart to heart. Man's mind, not his bodily frame, is the similitude of God; and mentality always was a social, not a solitary, thing. We learnt to talk, because they talked to us; and to like, because they smiled at us. Because we could first talk, we can now think; that is, we can talk silently to the images of the absent, or we can pretend to be our own twin, and talk to ourself.

I can talk to myself, but it is hard work. How easily (alas for my pupils!) does my speech flow when I talk to them; with what sorrow and reluctance did I drive myself when I was preparing this sermon, although it was for people who have given me as much reason to like them as any people alive, and although the subject is of all others most fascinating. Yet it was a labour to compose, simply because you were not there, but only the visionary ghost of you. I had to pretend you; it was the best I could do.

God does not have to pretend; that is where he differs from us. He speaks with himself; but the self with whom he speaks, and who takes the responsive part, is a dear and real person, the Son of his love. And what they exchange between them is no fragmentary expression of a passing thought, it is the whole mind and heart and substance of their godhead.

That is all Christians know about the life of God. We can weigh it, and turn it over, and phrase it a hundred ways; we can consider it in relation to a hundred things; can guard it against a hundred misconceptions. But it all comes down to this; this is all we know. And even then, as you will be quick to tell me, we cannot know it; it baffles understanding. We cannot think of different persons, unless they are identified with several lumps of flesh; still less can we conceive a thought so powerful, that it really constitutes the Other in the mind, instead of merely pretending him. And so we cannot think the Blessed Trinity. But then, it is not required of us to think the Trinity. We can do better; we can live the Trinity by grace of the Trinity.

As I have implied already, the life of the Trinity is represented

in us after two different fashions: in society with one another, and
in discourse with one's self. Each fashion of representation has its
special merit. Our society with our friends mirrors the reality of the
Trinity; it is real society and the persons involved in it are real
persons. A man's discourse with himself better represents the oneness of the Trinity: the divine Persons are as close to one another
as a man's own thought is to a man; yes, and closer than that.
Sometimes Holy Scripture speaks of a divine Father and a divine
Son; and that is to speak of a society between kindred beings.
Sometimes, on the other hand, Scripture speaks of God and his
Word; and that is to use the figure of a single mind and its uttered
expression. And I think you will find there are no other ways
Scripture does take beyond these two, in writing of that supreme
mystery.

It follows that we live the Trinity, in some sense, just by being
men; and it is no blasphemy to say that this dear Trinity of ours, in
all the companionship it engenders, or indeed, of which it consists,
is the offspring of the divine Spirit. More particularly in the special
work of a college, where the younger learn from the elder, and the
elder find happiness in the vitality of younger wits, you have an
enactment of the Blessed Trinity; a Trinity in which there is a
Father and a Son, and yet no disparity, but an equal delight of each
in each. But then again, it is specially characteristic of a college, that
our studies, with all accompanying sidelines of mental stimulation,
drive us to exercise in a more than trivial way that high privilege
of a rational being, to enter into converse with himself, and to beget
upon his own thought a new achievement of understanding.

Any man, then, who has the character to be either a thinker or a
friend lives the Trinity in some fashion, whether he is a Christian
or not. Has not God made us all in his own similitude? We can
achieve nothing truly human which is not also in a manner divine.
And we may wonder without end at the simple fact, that anything
so godlike as common friendship, or as ordinary rational discourse,
should be actualised in physical bodies. These things are the masterpieces of the Creator, and in these he delights.

And yet the Blessed Trinity has a higher delight in us, and we a
more heavenly partaking in the life of the Trinity, by our being
Christians. We may see how this is, if we recall that what the divine
Persons love in one another is not something that just happens to
be; it is the perfect truth of eternal godhead. The Father loves the

Son for perfectly expressing this; the Son adores the Father as the fount and archetype of all that his own being expresses. So Christians, in so far as they are Christians, like in their friends not what merely happens to be in them, good or bad; they prize in one another with a special regard what is sincerely good; that is to say, what expresses the goodness and the beauty of God. They see the will of God in one another's lives; they love the Creator Himself in his handiwork.

Or again, to speak of that other looking-glass of the Trinity, the discourse a man has with himself. That *alter ego* in the mind with whom we converse need not be the mere complacent shadow of our own desires, the bosom flatterer who is our own worst enemy: nor even the mere logical judge, the inner critic who forbids our getting away with dishonest argument. The Christian may go further; he may draw into converse with him an imagined other self who speaks for the very will of God. He may square his account with eternal truth and sovereign majesty, so far as he can find them in his heart, or see them bear upon his present life. Then suddenly he is not talking with himself at all, or with any system of his own imagining. The other person of his inward colloquy takes on the very name and character of the Creator. The principle of an eternal law warms with the kindness of a Father's care, encouraging us to speak with Him as sons. So a Person of the divine Trinity, the Father of Heaven, shows through one of the parties to our inner dialogue. But no sooner has this happened, than the other participant is similarly transformed. When we respond in filial duty to so heavenly a Father, our very self reveals the action, and expresses the person of his heavenly Son. Who does not know that when we genuinely pray, it is Christ who prays in us? And as for the bond of mutual liking which unites the two persons of our colloquy, it is no other than the inspiration of the Holy Spirit; for where the Father and the Son are, there is he.

What I have spoken of is no exalted mystical ecstasy; it is just praying, or even, without the form of prayer, any attending to the presence and will of our Creator. *Tota Trinitas illabitur menti*, the whole Trinity moves into the mind, says the great St Augustine, writing of this very thing. But we have better authority. 'We will come, and make our abode with him,' says the Christ of St John's Gospel. 'We'—that is, the Father and the Son, by the indwelling of the Holy Spirit. And with whom will they take up their abode?

With the man who 'will keep my words', says Christ; who guards
and honours by his obedience this treasure in the soul, this viceroy
of Heaven in the heart, the revealed thought and will of the godhead; a word able to come alive and to address us from the lips of
God, drawing us into that happy converse, which brings the Trinity
to earth, and raises earthly life to Heaven: where to the Triune
Sovereignty alone is, was and shall be ascribed, as is most justly due,
all might, dominion, majesty and power, in all eternity.

FAITH AND CRUTCHES

—preached in Keble College Chapel, Low Sunday, 1962

When the lesson for the day contains a really awful text, it seems mere cowardice not to preach about it. And what can be more shocking than this? *Thomas, because thou hast seen me, thou hast believed. Blessed are those, who have not seen, and yet have believed.* There are such aggravations of outrage here, one doesn't know where to begin, or where to end. But perhaps we can reduce the scandal to two sentences. First, our whole view of the world is to depend upon a physical miracle; Jesus, who died, has bodily returned. And second—as if that wasn't bad enough—the physical evidence, which would alone suffice to prove the physical miracle, is not to be asked for. Thomas, that sturdy-minded empiricist, has all our sympathies. If he can see, feel and explore, he is ready to be convinced: not otherwise. He has all our sympathies, but not the Evangelist's approval nor Christ's, either: blessed are those who have not seen, and yet have believed.

Did I say I would reduce the scandal to two sentences? I was over-hopeful: I must add a third. For, having apparently frowned upon Thomas for requiring signs in proof of faith, the Evangelist goes straight on to say that Christ worked many other signs beside the few wonders he has recorded in his gospel; but he has written those he has written, that his readers might believe, and have life in Christ's name through their faith. What are we to make of this? Miracles are to be the motives of our belief; and yet those who required the miracles to be shown, were at fault. It sounds as if St John was half ashamed of miracle, and yet cannot do without it. And even Christ himself, the Christ who speaks through his page—but no, he cannot be ashamed of miracle, unless he is ashamed of himself: for he is a walking miracle, the miracle of miracles, a man alive from the dead. And how can he be ashamed of the faithfulness of God which raised him, or ashamed of the compassion, which sent him back with speech on his lips and kindness in his eyes, to make himself known alive among his friends?

Perhaps, after all, we have not understood St John and our first false move was to moralise his story. We wanted to give good marks, and bad marks: Thomas was to have a bad mark for asking physical evidence, those content with hearsay were to have good marks. Or again, we wanted to talk the language of ought, and ought not: Thomas *ought not* to have required the evidence of his senses, hearing evidence *ought* to suffice. Look back once more at St John's text: you will find no foundation in it for such black-and-white judgements there. St John is black-and-white enough when the occasion calls for it. Israelites ought not to think they can advance God's cause by murdering the innocent. Men who begin to see a chink of spiritual light ought not to shut their eyes against it. St John is black-and-white enough on points like these. But he does not suggest that Thomas *ought not* to have required sense-evidence. When Thomas said to his fellow-disciples, 'unless I see and touch, I shall not believe', what do you think it was? Was it a refusal, or a boast, or a confession? A refusal—I won't believe: or a boast—I'm too clever to believe: or a confession—I shan't be able to believe? He was a friend and disciple of Christ's, who had risked his life with him: how could he refuse to believe that God had raised him from the dead? or how boast of sceptical detachment, who had committed himself to a cause, body and soul? No, surely it was more like a confession: That's the sort of man I am; I shan't be able to believe, unless I believe my own hands, and eyes. If, when he said this, Thomas was telling the truth, he could hardly have done better: do you think he would have done better if he had lied? If he had pretended to believe, when he didn't? When we come to Christ in our prayer, shall we tell him a pack of lies? Shall we pretend all sorts of noble sentiments we do not have: pretend to believe in him as firmly as we believe our own existence, pretend to care for his holy will as warmly and constantly as we care for our own comforts and ambitions? Of course not; for whom could we hope to deceive? Not him: we could only deceive ourselves. No, we will confess ourselves as we are, and know that he will treat us on our level, and according to our need, as he did Thomas: reach hither thy finger, and feel my hands; reach hither thy hand, and put it in my side; go not in lack of faith, but believe.

Jesus gave himself, that was all, and he gave himself to each according to his need, to each in his proper function; to Thomas into his arms to be handled and felt; to Peter and the rest to be seen, listened to, and conversed with; to the Church afterwards through the apostles' witness, and in the sacraments; in the lives of saints, and in the deaths of martyrs. He blesses those who are willing to let him make himself known in the way that he chooses; he blesses them, but he does not curse Thomas for his sense-bound mind and his physical demands. He does not curse him, no: what does he say? Reach hither your finger, and see my hands: take your hand, and put it in my side: and cure your unbelief.

But to return to St John's ambiguous attitude towards physical miracle. Except you see signs and wonders, you will not believe, says Christ to the frightened father, whose son was at the point of death. And again, at the raising of Lazarus; Christ is the resurrection and the life of men, whether he calls Lazarus from the tomb or not. What use does it serve, to bring back one dead man among so many millions: and then only that he may die again? Are not God's good purposes for us better fulfilled, when things follow their natural course: since we must die, is it not better to die once in faith, than to receive a violent resuscitation? Lazarus's return seems to be a concession to hardness of heart.

Christ's miracles were long ago, and perhaps you, like Thomas, do not easily believe them. If so—since you cannot travel back in time—you might like to consider some miracles more accessible to examination. Among many good ideas our Protestant reformers had, there were naturally some less good: and one of the most calamitous was the dogma that miracles ended with the New Testament. No doubt there was endless folly and credulity in the mediaeval Church, which needed to be pruned. But to deny all miracles of saints was to go in the face of evidence, and ultimately to destroy the grounds of belief. You might get hold of the life of the Blessed Curé d'Ars, who was not a mediaeval man, but was alive when my grandfather was born; and you will find it difficult to resist the evidence of his miracles, or indeed the supernatural character of his whole life. Yet his attitude to miracle was as ambiguous as Christ's attitude, or as St John's. There was one cripple in particular who pestered him for a cure. The saint preached at him time after time, to reconcile him to his condition. Since the doctors could not cure him, why would not he shoulder the common burden of his condition, and by his Christian patience offer a daily sacrifice, by which he could help his neighbours to bear their troubles and to love the will of God? The saint who told him this had a right to speak: he was himself a great sufferer, though he did not say so. It was all no good; the cripple could not accept his calling. 'Very well,' said the Saint, with tears in his eyes. 'Put your crutches in the corner, and walk out.' And he did.

That miracle is a concession to our condition who will deny? God will go no further in miracle, than we extort from him. But then the whole work that God did in Christ and still does for our salvation is a concession to our condition, extorted by our need for his compassion. Every line, every page, of the Gospel records the concession of divine wisdom to human folly.

'For look how high the heaven is in comparison of the earth: so great is his mercy also toward them that fear him. Yea, like as a father pitieth his own children: even so is the Lord merciful to them that fear him. For he knoweth whereof we are made: he remembereth that we are but dust.'

But for our sin, and our infirmity, he need neither have died, nor risen from the dead: that he did, we have every reason to rejoice, and to thank the mercy that has no end.

ROOTS IN GOD

It is now thought that poetry should be obscure—and so, of course, for the most part it is admired but not read. I will confess, whatever you may think of me, that I like to go back behind all that and to roll round my mouth one of the last of the English poets who would have been ashamed to be caught talking nonsense. For sheer clarity, for epigrammatic force, can you beat the two stanzas about the coward:

> My dreams are of a field afar
> And blood and smoke and shot.
> There in their graves my comrades are,
> In my grave I am not.
>
> I too was taught the trade of man
> And spelt the lesson plain;
> But they, when I forgot and ran,
> Remembered and remain.

What was biting the man? He couldn't keep off it—Housman couldn't forgive himself, it seems, for not having gone and got killed in the African War. Plainly it was a crime to survive—to stand up and die was the trade of man. That was one side of it. But then, on the other side, what was there in being shot? It was a thousand pities anyone should die young; they had not achieved their promise. Getting shot was a poor thing compared with living on to see the cherry trees break into blossom, and to write immortal verse. So there was Housman, hating life and hating death.

Being a more superficial sort of man than he, I cannot work up such a rage. As he says, we get on all right unless we think, and mostly one needn't think. But I can share his perplexity, when, looking back, I see myself sheltered from battle and sudden death, while the man I thought the best man of my acquaintance went to it. He was exempt by law from military service, he went a volunteer:

when his special skills would have placed him in the backroom,
then against the wishes of the command he would go to the firing-
line; and then, when they were advancing, he would reconnoitre the
ground ahead for himself, to spare his troops all possible danger.
And so he drew the fire of a hidden gun; and so he died. He died,
that man, just when he had reached the height of his powers. We
looked to him to achieve that miracle, a breakthrough of the Church
into the world of organised mass-labour. Like the disciples on the
road to Emmaus, we thought it was he who should have redeemed
our Israel. But being that sort of man, he got himself shot: just as
Christ, being what he was, got himself crucified. Others of us, not
being that sort of man, got ourselves a wide scope of further life,
but not being that sort of man, we have not done anything very
striking with it.

St Luke, who reports to us the disillusioned talk of the disciples
walking to Emmaus, tells us in another place that Jesus began his
public ministry at thirty years old, which the Jews regarded as the
age of first spiritual maturity: he was crucified (on any calculation)
within three years; a fact expressed by the original form of the best
hymn in our language:

> When I survey the wondrous cross
> Where the young prince of glory died.

On any human reckoning, he had shown infinite promise, and had
accomplished nothing. He had thrown out marvellous sayings, but
put no body of teaching in order. He had organised no regular
movement; he had left his followers raw and half-trained; he had
squandered his energy on lunatics and beggars; and then he had to
pull his death on his own head, for he could not stand by, not he,
and see his Father's house made a house of merchandise. But we
thought it was he who should have redeemed Israel; and when he
touched maturity, he died. No doubt, as the writer to the Hebrews
says, he learned obedience by the things he suffered, and was thus
made perfect, or mature; and the last thing he learned, was how to
die. But the trouble about learning the lesson of death is, that it has
no application: the man is dead. 'Yet we thought it was he that
should have redeemed Israel.'

'O slow of heart,' said the Stranger with the hooded face, 'O slow
of heart to believe all the prophets have spoken. Behoved it not

Messiah to suffer these things and so to enter his glory?' They came
to table; he took the bread between his hands, to bless it; and suddenly the glory burst upon them.

Jesus, who learned carpentry from Joseph, learned the trade of
man from his heavenly Father, in accepting his will, and making the
best of every occasion offered him. Ah, when shall I, when shall you,
learn the trade of men? The friend I spoke of just now—did he not
learn more in learning to squander his life, than we have learned in
hoarding ours? And when we have finished the study of life, what
shall we be found to have been studying for? When Jesus had
finished his education, he had nothing to wait for; he entered into
his glory.

When Jesus, just before his death, was asked about immortality,
he took the text, 'I am the God of Abraham, Isaac and Jacob': and
commented, 'He is not the God of the dead, but of the living.' There
is much food for reflection here. 'The God of Abraham, of Isaac,
and of Jacob'—patriarchal names: the names of men, whom the
childish faith of a previous generation had credited with almost
double centuries of years, that their earthly life might seem complete. God is their God; he wants them; but not, says Jesus, in that
rounded earthly existence. Jesus has taught us to say, 'Not the God
of Abraham, but the God and Father of our Lord Jesus Christ': and
Jesus died before he was thirty-five. God is the God *of Abraham*:
but what Jesus implicitly argues, is that Abraham is the Abraham
of God; and what is God's Abraham? not the patriarch ruling in his
family full of years and of honours, but the friend of God, redeemed
by fellowship with his maker, and fulfilled with glory.

Still we have not finished with the profundities of this marvellous
text. When Jesus quoted 'God of Abraham', he said he was quoting
from 'the Burning Bush', the chapter where God declares to Moses
his name and nature. And this, as every Israelite knows, he did in
double form: I (am) the God of Abraham and *I am that I am*. Those
who are rooted in God are rooted in being: the infinite energy of the
one creative act which God is comes back upon them and fulfils
them. They moulded a mortal vessel here by the life they lived and
the service they learnt: there they are filled with God as full as they
can hold.

Their roots strike into Being; but how deep? Abraham is the
friend of God—and what could one say more, than that God makes
man his friend, and shares his heart with us? But there is more—

if we will believe the Gospel of John: Abraham lived close on two hundred years, but Jesus, not yet fifty years old—the Jews complain—says he has seen Abraham. He replies: 'Before Abraham was, I am.'

And here we meet a strange comparison. Housman, whom I began by quoting, ends his poem:

> But they, when I forgot and ran,
> Remembered, and remain.

The whole effect is obtained by a grammatical jerk. What we expect is: when I forgot and ran, they, like good soldiers, remembered and remained—they stayed there to do their duty. But he says, *remain*: there they lie, removed out of the sequence of tenses into the timeless present of physical death.

So the Christ of St John's Gospel—he does not say (what would for the Jews already be far too much), before Abraham was, I was there—but, before Abraham was, I am. He has not been *associated by divine friendship* with the AM of eternal being; he has his simple share of it.

We have far more reason to veil our eyes before such a mystery than Moses had to turn his aside from the bush that burned and did not burn away. That a bush should be lighted with fire and yet unburnt was wonderful, but that our nature should be taken up into the first act of being, the AM of God's eternity and be still itself— what shall we say of that? So this was what was happening, in those thirty and more years of Christ's earthly life—the AM of everlastingness was possessing himself of a human history, fully learning the way of our human obedience by the things he suffered, and entering into every corner and cranny of our existence, down to death itself; that man might enter into glory, and Messiah be enthroned in heaven.

And this is the Gospel—that the partition veiling heaven from earth is as fine as paper. The Jesus who has entered into glory is God's Jesus, the Jesus for whose human nature God has done all that human nature can take, while remaining itself. But in becoming the Jesus of God he does not become any less the Jesus of Peter or of John; nothing was lost to God by his death, but nothing was lost to them either, if they had only the faith to live in that association, to be his men, to do his work, to listen to his Spirit.

And we are disciples too, heaven help us—and heaven will help us. There is nothing in God that is not mercy; and it is in our acknowledgement of that infinite compassion that we ascribe to the AM of everlasting life, the Father, Son, and Holy Ghost, all might, majesty and power, henceforth and for ever.

THE MAGNET OF GOD

—preached in Christ Church Cathedral, Oxford, 1967

Every age has its characteristic insights and its characteristic blind-spots. I dare say you'd agree with me that the spiritual insight characteristic of our time is a sense for the social function of religion. Social cohesion has never, perhaps, been weaker than it is in our artificial civilisation, and the sickness makes us value the remedy; religion at least creates community. So much for the insight. Now what about the blind-spot? Isn't it a lack of sense for the personal reality of God? Once again, our circumstances dictate our attitudes; and who is to blame us? The system of Nature on which we look out is so intricate, and above all, so vast, so inexpressive of living man-like purposes, that when we acknowledge a power behind it, we acknowledge we know not what. Doubtless, if we are to react in adoration to universal power, we shall have to sum it up, and set it before our minds in myths, symbols, personifications; and so, when we are in Church, we are prepared to hear the name of God. But out of Church, in the posture of cool reflection, we wonder whether God really has the personal character our prayers ascribe to him; or even, whether it (whatever it is) is really of a nature to justify our giving it the Name of God. Ought we to say 'God' except when we are talking pious poetry?

The question is of vital importance—unless—unless we are to be content with the sort of religion which can afford to discount it. And what sort of religion is that? It is a religion entirely made by us, a purely human affair; a pious reaction on our part to whatever reality there happens to be. But in this case, to talk about *faith* is moonshine: I cannot trust an unknown something with my life: I cannot love it: still less can it be supposed to love me.

Now since Christ and all the saints devoted themselves to the love of God, let us be perfectly clear that the merely symbolist account of theology must condemn them as completely misdirected and utterly deluded; we must reject their witness in every line. But then, on the other hand, how are we to talk ourselves into the belief

that infinite power has so human a face that we can look him in the
eyes and love him?

A terrible dilemma, one must admit; terrible, that is, for non-
Christian piety. But why should we Christians worry? To bring
God into dialogue with us we do not need to make the Universal
Cause our natural brother. God has anticipated us. God indeed, is
far other than man, but God has become man, so that he could meet
us. So long as he deals humanly with us, why should we trouble
ourselves as to what he is in himself?

Of course, if the unknown God puts on a human face to make
himself known among men, the act does reveal the unknown God —
he is no longer unknown altogether, even in his sheer divinity. The
Christian's last ditch of defence against sheer agnosticism is this:
God in his very being is personal enough, for it to make sense that
he should personify himself as man. 'It' cannot take flesh and live a
human life among us; the subject of such a condescension is not 'it',
but 'he'.

You might say to me, Why be an orthodox Christian? What a
narrow-minded position! You could be a pure theist, and be really
ecumenical. But I say, No. To be a pure theist is not, for me, a
genuine option. Unless God has gathered himself out of his immensity, and come to me as man, I do not even know that he is God —
not, that is, if by God you mean the object of a personal devotion.
Does the God of mere theism love the souls of men? And if he does,
how is it that he has left the immeasurable gulf between himself and
us unbridged? We cannot go to him. His love for us is that he comes
to us. So the divine incarnation is our all-or-nothing. It is a pity,
no doubt, that faith in Christ divides us from Jews and Turks; but
the acknowledgement of vital truth is always divisive until it becomes universal.

It is commonly supposed that the Incarnation of God is an old-
world belief, having no natural place in our times. It is commonly
supposed, but it is the very opposite of truth. In ancient unsophisti-
cated days, when God could be accepted as a manlike and virtually
finite being, there was the less need for an unique self-humanising,
self-finitising act on the part of infinite Godhead. It was the growing
perception of God's immeasurable transcendence which provided
the climate for his saving Incarnation. When the first Christians
looked back into the old-world stories of the Old Testament, and
saw the Almighty portrayed as visiting Abraham in his tent, under

the guise of a mysterious stranger, they did not know what to make of it. Surely, they said, this is a shadow of the coming Incarnation; for God in his divine majesty is not such a one as to be locally present or walk into any man's dwelling: he is our place—we cannot be his; in him we live, and move, and have our being. But the men who first told the stories had felt no such perplexities: they had not known that, in dealing humanly with his human creatures, the Creator moulds himself in mercy on the creaturely form and becomes as that which he has made.

So old religion assumed the self-humanisation of God without realising it. But now the issue is clear and open. Those who do not believe in it have a God remote from them; for present as he may be to them in power, he is as unseen as the air and there is no intercourse with him as of friend to friend. While we who acknowledge the Incarnation know a God supremely revealed in this act of effective and saving charity by which he becomes small that he may meet us and mortal that he may redeem us.

Christians have often been so overpowered by their sense of the divine presence in Christ, that they have seen him as no true man; a god in masquerade. But those whose imaginations have thus deluded them have been going flat contrary to the formal teaching of the Church, which acknowledges in Jesus Christ a manhood as entire as his deity. This was how God's love was shown as utterly divine—in accepting every circumstance, every limitation of our manhood. He spared himself nothing. He was not a copybook man-in-general, he was a Galilean carpenter, a freelance rabbi: and he wove up his life, as each of us must, out of the materials that were to hand. He found his way by groping and he knew his Father by trusting; only he made no false moves.

There is one aspect of Christ's true humanity which is not sufficiently remembered by Christians; and it is this, that humanity is a social fact: we need other men, to be human ourselves. What is our mind, but a dialogue with the thought of our contemporaries or predecessors? And what is our moral being, but a complex of relationships? You would be another man, if your friends, relations, and *bêtes noires* were different: and your personal being is profoundly altered if you deeply love a woman and go on in that companionship.

But have you reflected that Jesus was that Jesus because of Mary and Joseph and the village rabbi, a man to us unknown: above all because of the disciples to whom he gave himself and the poor people to whose need he ministered? But for these people, he would have been another Jesus. To be a man, he must have them, and to continue a man (as he still indeed is) he must retain them. So the life of God, incarnate in Jesus, cannot be locked within his breast; it becomes a spreading complex of personal being, centred in Jesus, and annexing his companions. Though we are each but a minute cell in the social body of Christ, yet, taking us in the lump and in the gross, he is what he humanly is by his relation to us.

And now I shall give you a definition of heaven. Heaven is a state of being, to us unknown, such that the obstacles to one man's knowing a multitude of individuals are done away. Then Christ is himself through taking us all into his heart and we shall be ourselves by taking him to ours.

So I return to my beginning. This age, I said, is specially sensitive to the cohesive qualities of religion. Cohesive—but how cohesive? By community-singing, organised activities and good fellowship; or by the action of their magnet, the life of God, thrust among the iron filings which we individually are, and drawing us into fellowship with eternal love, the communion of the Father and the Son in the Holy Ghost.

TRUE CHILD OF MAN

If I were writing a frivolous novel, and I wanted to be irreverent about a retired military officer, reading the lesson in a country Church, what passage should I choose? Would not it have to be one of those rather heavy-footed narratives from the Book of Daniel, say the Burning Fiery Furnace, or the Den of Lions, or the Madness of Nebuchadnezzar? One cannot help feeling that Hebrew story-telling reached a level of clumsiness and naivety here, which is in sad decline from the subtlety, the brilliance and the pathos of far earlier narratives, say those about David and Absolom, or Ahab and Elijah.

But if Hebrew story-telling had declined, Hebrew theology had greatly advanced; and the strength of Daniel lies in the province of symbols, and ideas: and what is exciting is the way in which the ideas and images run through from one vision or narrative to another. In fact, if the narratives are somewhat grotesque, it is because the author's attention is fixed precisely where a narrative writer's attention ought not to be—on the symbolism and on the moral. Nebuchadnezzar, though warned by Daniel to submit himself to the sovereign rule of God, went on in the pride of his heart, making himself the god of his empire, until in the midst of his mad boasting he was struck down; he fell on all fours and became a werewolf, or rather a wereox, and his embarrassed courtiers had no option—they turned him out to grass. After many seasons his reason returned; and his recovery of the human mind coincided with the blinding conviction that the heavens do rule. Well, stranger things have happened. I know a man who lived a most reckless and disorderly life and was a complete materialist. He got himself into a dangerous illness which deprived him of all rational consciousness. He was very strong, however, and recovered. The first reality he was aware of, before he could feel or see anything else, was the being of God. When he was well, he went to be a monk: he thought there was nothing else to do. They sent him out to me to do a bit of his theology. The man died years ago, in the war: else I would not tell you the tale.

So much for Nebuchadnezzar. He reformed; not so his successor, who took no warning by his father, but came to a swift and sticky end. Well, a simple story: not much in that. But wait. Presently Daniel dreams a dream. He sees the great idolatrous empires of the world under the figures of four beasts crawling up out of the deep below. One succeeds another, and the last has his day. The hour of revelation strikes: a prince in the human form—one like a child of man—comes down from above, and receives an everlasting empire, in which the kingdom of earth coincides with the kingdom of heaven.

Here at length the author's profound philosophy appears. Man, he sees, is an unstable creature, halfway between the god and the beast; he can only hold on to his humanity, by attachment to deity. By losing his hold on heaven, Nebuchadnezzar grovels to the earth; and in so doing he is a parable of all the empires and cultures which find it easy to deify themselves, because the gods they worship are no higher than their own heads. When a truly human empire comes to take their place, it is in the form of that Child of Man who reigns as the son and viceroy of God, the Ancient of Days.

These are old-world images, but the issues are contemporary enough. Have you heard of the humanists? Of course you have. Well, what is humanism? I am not sure, nor, I suspect are the humanists. It's an abstract noun, obviously, made out of the maxim, Be human. Humanism, like Liberalism, must command verbal assent: Who is going to say, No, thank you: I prefer to be illiberal? Or who is going to say, Be human? Certainly not! Let's all be as inhuman as possible. Political liberalism has a special recipe for being liberal, and humanism will have to have a special recipe for being human, if its troops are going to march in any one direction rather than in any other. Otherwise they will be like the Roman soldiers in the stage farce, who sing a marching song about their yearning for Rome, sweet Rome, but keep about turning and marking time, because they are at a cross-roads, and all roads lead to Rome. So all human roads lead to human objectives; which shall the humanists take?

Well, what is a humanist in practice? On the one side he is concerned to guard against the folly of building up machinery supposed to be of service to men, but which in fact impoverishes or enslaves their existence. Don't forget the end, he says, in your elaboration of the means. Machines may be useful, but man alone is valuable.

Splendid. We can all be humanists along these lines. But the next step is more controversial. Not only is humanity the aim, but man is the master. Who and What, say the humanists, is to stop men from getting together, deciding what is good for them, and doing it in concert? This, so far, is once more a harmless platitude. No one can be anything—no one can be a Christian, even—apart from his own will and decision; certainly it is very clear that Christ did not, and does not, want any but free and willing disciples.

But humanism is often taken to mean, that man is not only the master of his decision; he is to make that decision without reference to any other being than the human being, whether it be his own, or other men's. Here, of course, Daniel disagrees. It is only by acknowledging that the heavens bear rule, that Nebuchadnezzar can preserve the human image at all: by setting up as his own god, he becomes a beast. Now it is a sound rule that we should free ourselves from dependence on what is alien to us, but it is lunacy to free ourselves from what is native to us; it is no freedom to get away from dependence on the air we breathe, or (we that are students) from dependence on the sources of information, or any of us from dependence on our friends for our happiness. Now (says Daniel) what is man? He's an animal—a beast—into whose nostrils has been breathed a breath of the divine Spirit, and he lives by coming up to breathe, like a diver—to breathe the air of the divine kingdom.

Enough of generalities. What is the practical issue among members of the University? Sex, as they now call it—they used to call it love: but that just shows the way things are going. And what is sex (especially when called by that name)? Just an animal function: what else? Well, how do you *humanise* it? The difficulty is considerable: for man, through the possession of thought and fancy, can outdo the beasts in bestiality; we know how, through the unscrupulousness of advertisers and entertainers an atmosphere of erotic obsession can be generated, to which animals could never be liable. So the Christian recipe for being human is to make sex the physical basis of a monogamous marriage, and the expression of a lifelong devotion; and to stabilise chastity by making it a devotion to God.

So the Christian says he is the true humanist, and he is sad, though not surprised, to see those who deny that the heavens bear rule going out to grass with Nebuchadnezzar.

The ancient classics, we know, are often a somewhat obscene

study, but at least they are a wholesome warning. No one can become familiar with the ancient world and especially the Roman world without seeing what happens when sex takes the place of love —what a terrible waste of moral energy, what a brutalisation of human relationships. But God had mercy on that bestial world, and sent the Son of Man.

For, after all, the importance of Daniel's tales and visions does not lie in themselves, but in the use Christ made of them. Of all the titles available for his use in the Jewish traditions, he chose this emblem of Daniel's child of Man descending with the clouds of heaven. Jesus restored the human image, because he brought down the divine: and no one knew how human man could be, until the king of heaven came to earth, and Christ was born of Mary.

GATES TO THE CITY

Amazingly generous people, the Americans; go over there, and you will see. They will not even let you buy a box of matches, they shower them for nothing. A card of matches is thrown in with your packet of cigarettes; every sort of business stamps its own with its title or monograph, and is proud or happy to present them to its clients. One gets used to the treatment. I was somewhat taken aback, however, to find on my table an unusually large and handsome card of matches, bearing the insignia of the Tranquilla Funeral Home, and offering, on the underside of the flap, the accommodation of three chapels with ample parking space to a delighted public.

It is curious, when you think of it, that death should be a joke; for death, indeed, is no laughing matter. But then, that is the joke — death is no laughing matter, and yet some complaisant little man, driving a trade in the funerary business, shows off a mortuary with a salesman's smile, as one might advertise a tea-shop. Not only is this a joke; it is the classic formula of comedy. Your comic writer lets loose the great forces of passion or of destiny; only to show his characters responding to them with a ludicrous triviality. Then, by a series of expedients, he preserves the threatened equilibrium; nothing happens after all, and the gulf which so nearly yawned for us is skimmed over in the insincere prattle of a drawing-room.

All the same, the death-joke comes uncomfortably near the bone, and almost breaks the comic formula. If someone dies, it is difficult even to pretend that nothing of consequence has occurred. Oscar Wilde, dying (as he said) beyond his means, might talk about death as the running of a bill. The frivolity only pointed the pathos — he was dying, poor chap.

Tragedy takes the opposite path; the full force of the dangers threatening our comfort are disclosed, and they are allowed their maximum effect. Lear drinks to the dregs the cup of his folly; Hamlet's experiment in just vengeance makes an awful bloody mess; no undeceiving circumstance turns Othello from the road of murderous jealousy.

It has often been remarked that Tragedy, though certainly more disturbing, is also more consoling than Comedy. For while it is amusing to see the threats of existence sidetracked into anti-climax, it is not altogether reassuring. We are left with the disquieting reflection that things might just as well turn out otherwise; and what then? Tragedy does not load the dice in our favour, but lets us see that even when the worst happens, mankind can face it in some sort of fashion.

To turn from the stage to the world, we observe the same kind of awful satisfaction in war. Peace is a balancing-trick which, we fear, is bound some time to collapse. War is a showdown, and then we know where we are. We did not know where we were in 1940, not until all the forces were engaged on either side. The Italians, the Russians, the Japanese, the Americans had all to be drawn in; the last shackles of civilised convention had to be thrown off. When total war, when global war had been fought out, we should know where we were then. And so we did, no doubt; but only for the moment. That is the fault in political affairs: there is no finality. No sooner is war finished, then we patch another peace, and in a few months we know no better where we are, than we did before.

Unlike Churchill's victory—or, to please our Russian friends, let us say, unlike Stalin's—Christ's triumph was final. All the more reason why the showdown should be complete. It was our battle he was to win, not a private war of his own. The cruel deity of circumstance must not be allowed to pull her punches. He must sound the very depths, if he was to scale the heights. 'That he ascended,' says St Paul, 'what is it but that he descended first into the lower parts of the earth?' In the visible realm, anyhow, he was spared nothing. 'He became obedient unto death,' says the same Apostle, 'and that death, the death of the cross; wherefore also God highly exalted him.'

He was spared nothing in the visible realm; but not in the invisible either. When he died, he did not wake from a bad dream, and find he was God. He went lower yet; descended into hell, says our creed. That is, he died, and he was dead. For hell, in this formula of words, means simply this: whatever is the condition of the dead, when they have died.

And what condition is that? What is it to have died, and to be dead? If resurrection is unimaginable, how much more unimaginably unimaginable is death? Resurrection will refashion us in the

stuff of glory. We shall not be flesh and blood, but we shall be ourselves, and anyhow, we shall *be*. But death, what is death? What is
the tenuous thread which spans the abyss of not-being, to join our
being what we were with our being what we shall become? This
stretch, this nakedness, this expectancy, what is it? I do not know,
but Christ knows; for he descended into hell.

The Son of God became man in Christ. We generally think that
it happened on Lady Day, or perhaps at the first Christmas. And
yet an embryo is but the seed of manhood, and infancy little more
than the promise of it. Are children human, before they can speak?
And when they have spoken, how long is it before their words or
their wills are their own? Christ became progressively a man by
everything he did or suffered, up to the peak of his maturity. Then,
in the flower of his age, he died. When he died, his making was not
finished; for what sort of a man was he to remain? Not the sort of
man we are, nor the sort of man any of us have ever seen, but the
sort of man we must each of us be one day by God's grace; not
the man in flesh and blood, but the man in glory. And how was he
to reach that state? How is anyone to reach it, anyhow while this
world lasts? He must pass the dead point of Hades. The parallel
rays of the sun, passing the lens of a burning-glass, are so deflected
that they slope together and cross all in a single point, a point, ideally
speaking, with no magnitude; which point being passed, they fan
out again into a fresh cone. The cone spreads to light, and, were it
unbroken by any obstacle, should expand to all infinity. Death, the
annihilation of all we were, is the point of no magnitude into which
our being must contract, if it is to expand into the flower of glory.
This is the pinpoint, this is the needle's eye, which we must pass to
enter the kingdom of Heaven. Here the rich unloads his wealth, and
the proud his state, yes, and the poor his skin and bones, to slip
through into a better world.

'Lift your lintel-heads, you gates: raise yourselves, you age-old
portals', cried Israel before the entry of the temple, where in ritual
procession the King of Glory was to go in. The Church applies the
words to Christ's entry of heaven. Heaven itself is not enough to
contain him; and this is something more than poetry, for what is
heaven? It is nothing but Jesus Christ, and those in union with him.
If angels and archangels were heaven before Christ's glorious manhood ascended there, heaven was not heaven enough, there was no
place in all its places great enough for Christ. Heaven was a hundred

7

times raised, and stretched, and glorified when a person passed its gates, who was the ark and shrine of Almighty Godhead. And so Christ says at the Supper. 'I go to prepare a place for you.' Indeed, by entering there, he makes all the place there is: place for all whose common humanity can hang on the skirts of his glory, or be presented by Jesus before the Father of Jesus.

The gates of heaven, the whole wall and compass of the city are stretched when Christ enters there. Not so the door of death. He is made as little, as low, as mere a nothing as any dying man, when he passes that door. That he ascended, what is it but that he descended first into the lower parts of the earth? We fall on our knees in the creed, to honour the condescension of Almighty God, when he came down from heaven, and was made man in the womb of Mary, by the Holy Ghost. We do not kneel again in the solemn profession of our faith, and perhaps we think the Incarnation was the lowest point, as though from there onwards Christ mounted step by step the stair of heaven. Are we not wrong? Was not he still on the way down, plunging into the depth of our condition, until he reached the grave and the death? Is not it a more profound humiliation to be incarnate in death than in any life, however rudimentary, however embryonic?

Christ came down that he might ascend, and ascending take us with him. Every part of our human course is attached to him, at no point does he leave us. We can live with him, we can die with him; we can be dead with him that we may rise with him. We may not have begun with him, we can catch on at any point. Christ was a child, and so children may be in Christ. Yet many who were not children in Christ become men in Christ by a later conversion. Manhood, even, may not be in Christ, and yet old age may come to know him. And it was in the thought of the ancient Church, that hope does not end there, either. Where life has not been attached to Christ, death may be; not for those, perhaps, who, living, lacked good will; who heard the Gospel with living ears, and turned from it by their own fault. Not, it may be, for them. But there are a million million souls who could not be Christ's in their life time, and yet who passed the test of the everlasting shepherd, by which he promises himself to divide the sheep from the goats. They fed the hungry, they clothed the naked, and so doing embraced the Son of God in his appointed deputies. For all such, Christ's ascent is the heavenly ladder. The bottom rung stands in the very cave of death and world of shadows. When Christ goes up, death is emptied of its people. The gates of Sion may well lift their arches and widen their ways, to admit so vast a company.

Where our steps will one day go, our aspiration goes before. Today, offering this holy sacrifice, we are one with Christ, and all the host of heaven. We lift our hearts on high, we pray with Christ the prayer of Christ; and Christ comes down in sacramental presence, to take us into the heaven which he is. Can we but pray in his mind, we pray the prayer which cannot be refused. What shall we ask? Each knows the burden of his own soul, and we share in common the burden of the world. Bread, we cry, bread for the starving, peace for the terrified, love for the hard of heart, life for the departed, and Christ for all.

THE LEGACY

—preached in Pusey House, Oxford, 1968

When Jesus died on the cross, says St John, there came away three things from his body; breath, blood, and water. He bowed his head, and breathed out his life. They ran the spear through his side, and there flowed out water and blood. The fact can be physiologically interpreted, but that's not what interests St John, as we see when we turn to his first epistle. What, he then asks, is the present and living evidence of the Gospel? The evidence is threefold, he says: the breath, the water and the blood. The threefold legacy of the dying Christ is alive in the Church to which he bequeathed it. It is set out in his sacramental gifts: his water is their baptism, his breath the spirit of their confirmation; his blood the wine of their chalice. Well, a Christian may say so: but how should the esoteric ceremonies of the Christian congregation be what St John says they are—God's evidence to the world, a testimony which nothing but wilful blindness could resist? Why, because the sacramental realities fill the life of the Christian. The water stays with them—they are pure; the breath breathes through them—they are inspired; the blood is in their veins and they are ready to be martyrs. *There* is the witness of the breath, the water and the blood. St John's doctrine is merely summarised in the Jesuit prayer for everyday:

> Breath of Christ hallow me
> Body of Christ keep me
> Blood of Christ inflame me
> Water from Christ, wash me

A church in which these aspirations were sincere, and these petitions granted, would be the Church of St John, instinct with the threefold witness of the breath, the water, and the blood. St John's Ephesians did not hold meetings to see how they could galvanise themselves into a mission: they were a mission and the Gospel ran like wildfire, as we are historically assured, up the Anatolian coast.

Of the triple witness, two strands are plain enough. If Christian lives were pure, they were pure: if the blood of the martyrs ran, it ran. So much for the water and the blood. But, St John tells us, the breath is also an evidence, a palpable fact—the Christians are inspired, you can't gainsay it. And what sort of a fact is it? What *is* life in the Spirit?

Well, have you encountered it? If you have, we needn't waste time on definitions. John Locke, we remember, offers us the definition of a certain substance as being a metal, yellow, heavy, ductile, malleable, fusible and fixed, and soluble in *aqua regia*. Many thanks for the definition, John: and now please hand me a bit of the stuff, and I shall know what you are talking about. Oh, it's *gold*, is it? And if you have had the true metal in your hands—have known a Christian alive in the Spirit, or ever made the acquaintance of such a being through his writings, look at him, don't look to me. For my part I'll fix my eyes on one or two specimens and report what I observe: and you can check from your own observations.

My spiritual man—may I call him Angelicus?—is characterised less by enthusiasm or visible zeal, than by self-forgetfulness. He has strong and persistent desires, or concerns, indeed, but they are not about himself. Neither are they specially about me; and that is vexing. I wanted Angelicus to be my friend, and so he was, in a way: he gave himself completely to me when the two of us were together; but when there were others present his heart was just as much with them. I wrote him the most amazing letters, and he answered them pleasantly. Pleasantly but shortly; I'm sure he wrote much longer and more frequent letters to the most tedious people, if they happened to be in any sort of worry or to need bolstering up. Call that friendship? It was maddening: he even seemed to like the wretched creatures. Why, he might just as well have been God himself: Angelicus, the man with the God's eye view—only that suggests an Olympian survey, from a great height; say a God's eye view if God's eye were right down on the floor, and just behind everyone's head, and inside everyone's mind at once, if you can imagine such a thing. Oh, but it is, isn't it? Yes, of course, you're perfectly right: the eyes of the Lord do run through the whole earth.

The God's eye view is seeing everything for what it is, and loving it for what it's worth. And that, I suppose, is what you'd call spiritual-mindedness. But when one's said that, one still hasn't got Angelicus. It isn't just that he is spiritual-minded: he's more than that—he's inspired; his spiritual-mindedness, if you see what I mean, goes with a whizz. How shall I put it? You and I, when we pray, climb up a few inches out of our selfish and worldly little bodies and take a look round in God's larger air, and it's wonderful, and exhilarating, though a bit difficult to breathe. We think a few noble thoughts, and make a few decent resolutions; but we can't struggle free. We acknowledge some extra duties, which we perform with pain, and place a few restraints on ourselves, which we observe with reluctance. There we are, stuck half in our bodies and half out: hadn't we better plunge right back into flesh and be hearty animals? This half in, half out, is an awful business. What I would, that I do not: wretched man that I am, who shall deliver me from this body of death? But Angelicus—he's out and away: what God loves is lovely to him; he's up and after it.

The true Christian is inspired. Don't waste your time wondering whether his inspiration falls in the province of psychology or of divinity. The psychological processes through which a free concern for God's will rises in the heart need have nothing special about them; it's the same old heart-strings thrumming away, even when they are playing a divine music. Life in the Spirit manifests itself in very various forms of psychological spontaneity, but psychological spontaneity, as such, is not life in the spirit: only such spontaneity as gives rein to heavenly-mindedness. This is a very old piece of Christian wisdom. Test the Spirits, says St John, whether they be of God. And the touchstone of their genuineness lies not in how they seem to come, it lies in what they say.

When St Paul cries out for wretchedness and asks who shall deliver him from his corpse of a body, he goes straight on to give God thanks for Christ the Lord, through whom he obtains that deliverance: for it is Christ who actually brings him into the vivifying stream of the divine life. The life and act of God is indeed, everywhere, but as poor Job complained, it is another matter to follow the veins and find the pulses of it. The life of God is everywhere, for the Creator everywhere descends into his creation and goes along with every one of his creatures by knowledge, by concern, and by action. To live in the Spirit is to go with God; but how shall I go with him, unless Christ sets me on the way?

In the Supper discourses in St John's Gospel, Christ promises the Paraclete as a second self, as an overflow of Christ. But, as that gospel makes clear, Christ himself lived first in the very overflow of God.

Angelicus is no more than an expression of Christ; Jesus is the very
man who lives outside himself, who lives in the Spirit.

The primitive Christians, who read their Bibles very simply in
Greek, found verses in the Old Testament which leapt at them from
the page in letters of flame. For instance they found this in the Book
of Numbers. What is to be done, asks Moses of the Lord, to shepherd Israel when he has passed away, lest they scatter like a leader-
less flock? And the oracle of God replies: take Jesus,* the man in
whom is the Spirit, and put your hands on his head . . . Jesus, the
man in whom is the Spirit; Jesus, the vessel of the Holy Ghost;
Jesus who goes outside his animal being, to make the heart and eyes
of God his own. When Jesus left his village setting, and made the
family of God his family, 'we must go and get him,' said his kindred,
'for he's jumped out of his skin,'—and how right they were, except
that there had been no jump. Jesus had never been inside his skin as
ordinary human animals are, pent in this body of death. He had
lived in a larger air: he had been in the Spirit of God.

It was by being outside himself—by being ecstatic in the literal
sense of that word that Jesus brought the life of the Blessed Trinity
into our world; for it is in ecstasy and in mutual indwelling that the
marvellous life of the Godhead consists, God Our Father goes out
of himself to be all in his Son—this is the first ecstasy: and the Son
goes out of himself to live by that very indwelling of the Father in
him—that is the second ecstasy. There is a third ecstasy when there
is a creation, and God comes out of himself to be all and everywhere
and all things in his creatures. It is the fourth ecstasy, when the
creatures of God go out of themselves to be in the God who in-
dwells them. But this ecstasy the creatures of God scarcely achieve,
until the Son of God takes on the form of a creature, and lives
therein the ecstatic life: and when he died on the cross, he gave it to
us for a legacy. Then he made his will, as he hung a-dying: he gave
Mary to John, and John to Mary; he left us the breath, the water
and the blood. We come here to claim the legacy of Christ. Ah,
how much more he longs to give, than we to claim. May his very
love release us from the body of this death.

*Joshua (Hebrew) = Jesus (Greek).

A SHARE IN THE FAMILY

—for All Saints Day

There is an Indian story which I suppose everyone has heard—the story of the wolf-children. From time to time a shewolf who has lost her cubs picks up human infants from a village cradle, carries them off and suckles them. Years later they are found again by the villagers, running with the wolfpack and behaving like wolves. There is nothing human about them except their shape. So far the story is always the same story: from this point on the several versions diverge. Sometimes the tale is, that the wolf-children can never be humanised; sometimes it is, that they are slowly and with difficulty educated into being men.

The story of the wolf-children is an unsolved puzzle. Our learned doctors say the thing's impossible, because human infants cannot survive a week on a diet of wolf's milk and raw meat. On the other hand, there are plenty of witnesses to the fact, among others a pair of much-respected Christian missionaries. It's a strange business. Never mind; even if the tale is an invention it's an intelligent invention: it expresses the truth, that without other people we just can't be human. We all lay like idiots in the cradle; and idiots we should have remained, if no one had smiled us into smiling back, or talked us into talking. And if we could have been brought up by wolves, they could have made nothing better than wolves of us.

Christians sometimes talk about Jesus Christ, as though he had walked down from heaven a readymade man, with a complete outfit of true ideas in his head; as though he had only pretended to be a babe in the cradle. But he made a more thorough job of being human than that; he needed a mother to smile at him, a father to talk to him, if he was ever going to be a man. Without Mary and Joseph he wouldn't have been anyone on earth. The divine life came to earth in Jesus, he was the heart and centre of it: but the divine life could not live or act in Jesus alone. The divine life had to use his parents, his kindred and his friends, to make Jesus a man;

and had to use his disciples and associates to keep him being a man; for we cannot go on being human, any more than we can get to be human, without other people. What is a painter without colours, brushes, or canvas to use? What is a teacher, without pupils or disciples to pull the wisdom out of his heart? And what can a Saviour be, without souls to attach to God, by attaching them to himself? Jesus could only be Jesus, by having Peter, James and John to be himself with; and he would have been a different Jesus, if he had had different associates, just as you would be a different person, if you were married to a different wife or husband. Jesus became the saviour of his friends, by attaching them to himself: but the attachment was mutual. When it came to his hour of trial, he did not want to be alone; he took them with him when he prayed in Gethsemane, he begged them to keep awake and see him through his agony of spirit. Some of them tried to get near him in the court when his case was heard; Mary and John even stood by his cross. Yet his death, like everyone's death, was solitary: no one can take that last step along with us. Our friends may stand around us, but we shall very likely neither see nor hear them. The moment when we cease to be what we were is the moment which cuts us off from company. But the moment when we become what we are to be, the moment of new life, of resurrection, restores us to fellowship with the living: and Jesus was no sooner risen from the dead than he was among his disciples. He was the first to die of the divine fellowship. Since none of his human friends were in heaven, no wonder if he came to find them on earth.

Jesus was more of a man, not less of one, by having died and risen; he needs men not less, but more, if he is to continue his divinely human life; for now his range of fellowship is unlimited, he spreads himself over mankind.

It was only a matter of months, it seems, until Stephen followed Jesus, and died a martyr; then James—and Mary died, we do not know just when. And so the friends of Christ in Paradise built up to a great company, and meanwhile his friends on earth did not decrease but constantly added to their numbers. Still Jesus is only Jesus by what his friendship does in human souls, whether those souls are on earth or in heaven. In heaven—for naturally, those who are joined in one life and action with the Son of God cannot die. How should they die? As Jesus said to Martha, distressed for the death of her brother Lazarus, 'I am the Resurrection and the Life:

he that believeth in me, though he die, shall live; and he that liveth and believeth in me, shall not die eternally.'

St Paul, seeing that the friends of Christ are one life with Christ, used a very bold figure of speech; he said that Christ and we are all one body, Christ the head, we the various limbs of it. Sometimes he used a bolder figure still, and said that we are all one Christ. And yet St Paul knew well—no one knew better, that he was a sinful man, a victim to pride and to wayward desire. His part in Christ's body of life—our part in it—is by the overflowing generosity of Christ, who treats us as being what he makes us. We are not the body of Christ because we are good men, but because Christ works in us to make us so.

There is a question I would like to put to you. If ever you come to Holy Communion on a Saint's day, what do you make of it? The collect mentions the saint, and, if he was a martyr, recalls his heroic death. But then, as we go on in the service, we set aside the martyr and his martyrdom; we commemorate a death in bread and wine, but it is the death of Jesus that nourishes us. Where does the martyr come into it? Wouldn't it be better to commemorate him by himself in a different sort of service?

I answer, No. A martyr is only a martyr because his sacrifice was the act of Christ in him, and a saint is only a saint because his life is the life of Christ in him. All the feast days of the saints are feast days of Christ—of the Christ in Francis or the Christ in Bernard or the Christ in Paul. They are what they are by feeding on Christ, just as we feed on Christ; having union with Christ in the Holy Sacrament we have union with all his people, all his mystical body.

And above all, the Feast of All Saints is a feast day of Jesus Christ, the feast of all his glorious actions in the whole body of the people he saves. Sometimes we hold a feast in honour of a public performer—a great singer or dancer. We seat him or her by the head of the table, we hear handsome speeches, we drink the toast in wine. It is all very well, but it's an indirect sort of way for showing the distinction of a dancer or a singer. Oh, for heaven's sake, says somebody, let him stand up and sing! Let her stand up and dance! Then in the perfection of the action, in the delight of our ears and eyes, the glory of that person would appear.

So if we are to feast the glory of Jesus—let our imaginations place him in the high seat of heaven, let us raise anthems in his honour. Yet it's an indirect sort of way for showing a Saviour's glory: for heaven's sake, let him stand up and save! There is no need to bid him do so: see how the vigour of his saving love works through the length and breadth of earth and heaven, how countless lives live by the bonds that tie them to his heart, how his Spirit stirs their minds, his love looks out of their eyes!

Where Jesus is, there is the Communion of Saints: his life never lives, his action never acts, alone: he gives his saints everywhere a part in all of it. Jesus gathered his disciples round him in Gethsemane to pray with him, and they fell asleep. Unsleeping, his saints pray with him in glory, where their whole life becomes a prayer; a holy desire, strong and efficacious, for the fulfilment of Christ's redemption, and the accomplishment of his kingdom; a perfect union of heart and mind with the society of love, of Father, Son and Holy Ghost, three persons in one God.

WALKING SACRAMENTS

—preached in Holy Trinity, Northwood, at Edward Ryan's First Mass, on the evening of 22 December 1968

The Gospel for today shows us John the Baptist under fire. People want to know what he claims to be. They are not content to take his message on its merits. If they rally round him, round whom or round what will they be rallying? Round a man called John, certainly, the son of a priest called Zacharias. Anyone could know that much. But what is this man John? According to Jewish rules he is a priest, because the son of a priest was a priest himself. But all a Jewish priest could do was take his turn at ceremonial duties in the Temple at Jerusalem. And here was John, calling people out from Jerusalem into the wilderness, to consecrate themselves in readiness for a great act of God, a divine event which would involve them all. What right had he to do it? In the past God had given them a King, who had a first claim on their loyalty, being the Lord's anointed; and though the Kingdom had fallen, God had promised to revive the dynasty of David. Was John the promised King of glory? He said he was not: nor was he the promised Prophet, the second Moses; nor yet the reborn Elijah, who must come before Messiah the King. What then? John must say something about himself. He must pin himself down to some fixed position in the great unfolding purposes of God. He must claim some function conferred on him by God's own hand. And so he does, but he makes the humblest, the least pretentious claim which will meet the case. I am, he says, simply that herald-voice which, in Israel's prophecy, proclaims the coming of the Lord. I run, shouting, before his advance, that all may be ready to receive him. But when he comes to his inn, and turns in to lodge, my work is done: I am not fit to kneel before him or ease his travel-worn feet by taking off his sandals. Nevertheless, for all his unpretendingness, John is the heaven-sent herald, he has a place in the scheme of things which obliges all believing men to rally round him and accept his ministry.

John was under fire, he was called on to explain himself: and so it is with the Christian priest today. People want to know what he is, and what he claims to be. Like John, he has a message to deliver, but that's not enough: you want to know why you should pay him any particular attention. Why listen to a clergyman giving you his views on life in general? A student of politics will be more topical, and a philosopher will be more profound. He would be wise, you might think, to stick to theology and Bible-learning. But though he has certainly had some special training there, he has no monopoly. There is nothing to stop a layman from being a more learned and a more penetrating theologian than the priest of his parish; nothing, certainly to prevent a layman from being a much more understanding helper of people in any sort of trouble or sorrow. So when the Christian priest is brought under fire, like John the Baptist, what is he to say of himself? What *is* he when we come down to essentials? What distinctive place does he hold in the mighty purposes of God?

The answer is before your eyes. Here is a new-made priest, and what does he do? He hastens to the altar: he sets forth the mystery of love, the body and blood of Christ, in bread and wine.

You know what is the special mercy of Christ to us in the Sacraments. It is, that he just puts himself there. He does not make it depend on anything special in us who receive, certainly not in anything special in the bread and the wine; nor in anything special about the priest either, except just that he is a priest. That's the essential point. Apples don't drop from the sky, they grow on apple trees. And sacraments don't hurtle down here and there like lightning from heaven: they grow on the great branching tree of the Apostles' ministry, the tree planted by Christ when he called twelve men and made them his ambassadors; a tree which has grown and spread and thrown its arms out all through history, to fill the whole earth. Into which tree, by virtue of his ordination, every new priest is grafted.

So, then a priest is a living stem, bearing sacraments as its fruits: he gives you the body and blood of Christ: he gives you, if you faithfully confess before him, Christ's own absolution. And that's not all; the man who bears the Sacrament is sacramental himself; he is, one might almost say, himself a walking sacrament. He is the appointed flag for Christ's people to rally round: the centre of unity to which we hold in every place. Just exactly what a priest is, you can see best in the Holy Eucharist. In a great part of that holy action he is, of course, no more than the voice of the congregation. Some of the prayers we say with him, some we let him say for us:

it makes little difference. Or again, in receiving the sacrament, the priest is in the same position as any other Christian, receiving the body and blood of Christ. But there is a moment when the priest steps into the place of Christ himself, to do what Christ did, to bless and to break, to present the mysterious sacrifice before God Almighty. It is much the same in absolution. If you have gone and made your own confession to the priest, you will understand what I say, when I tell you that Christ speaks in him the absolving words.

These moments, certainly, are exceptional in the activity of a priest; exceptional, but still not disconnected with his whole life or character. The man who is as Christ in the Sacrament is not just like anyone else ever: he bears the stamp. He is always, as I said before, a sort of walking sacrament, a token of Christ wherever he is: in him Christ sets up the standard of his kingdom and calls us to the colours.

It is just this fact that shows up the priesthood so terribly, and makes us, and them too, so painfully aware of their deficiencies. No one's calling or profession shows them up as a priest's does. And indeed, as I began by saying, there is nothing to prevent a priest from being a very ordinary man; most priests must always have been so. Being a priest does not make a man more helpful to his fellow-Christians in matters of wisdom or of kindness; what it does do is give his fellow Christians a right to his services. It might well be (to take another case) that the woman next door to you had greater gifts for teaching small children than the school-mistress: but that doesn't mean you can expect her to teach your little family for you. You've a *right* to the school-mistress's services; she's given herself over to be eaten alive by the children of the place. And so with the priest: go on, eat him alive, it's what he's for; you needn't feel shy of devouring his time, so long, of course, as it's to fulfil a need.

Or again, in matters strictly of religion. Anyone may be a better Christian than the priest, more holy of life, more deeply versed in prayer. But the priest has a special obligation to lead a devout life, to study divinity, to pray; and so to be fit to give some help to his fellow-Christians in these supremely important concerns. Other people may expound the faith, and speak or write in Christ's name, more wisely and more competently than the priest. They *may* do such things, and even do them better; the priest *must*: he must keep the congregation supplied with its staple diet: he must keep giving them some word from God.

I've been talking all this while (have I not?) about the priesthood as 'they', as though I wasn't one of them. But of course I am, and I've been thinking about my own office. And as I talk to you I hope that you will be listening to me as to a priest—that is, you won't just be pulling my (no doubt inadequate) remarks to pieces, but that you'll be listening for something from the voice of God, spoken over my shoulders; for God commends to you, surely, his new-made priest, for you to take him to your hearts; to receive from him the blessings with which he has been entrusted, and to make him your common friend.

There is inevitably something absurd about our priesthood, because what we stand for is so infinitely greater than our poor little selves. But there's the same absurdity, really, about being a Christian at all. None of us can be let off being Christ in our place and our station: we are all pigmies in giants' armour. We have to put up with it: it's the price (how small a price!) paid for the supreme mercy of God, that he does not wait for our dignity or our perfection, but just puts himself there in our midst; in this bread and this wine: in this priest: in this Christian man, woman, or child.

He who gave himself to us first as an infant, crying in a cot, he who was hung up naked on the wood, does not stand on his own dignity. If Jesus is willing to be in us, and to let us show him to the world, it's a small thing that we should endure being fools for Christ's sake, and be shown up by the part we have to play. We must put up with such humiliation of ourselves, or better still, forget ourselves altogether. For God is here: let us adore him.

INTO THE HANDS

—preached in St Mary's, Primrose Hill, Advent 1959

There is a primitive, not to say savage, story in the Second Book of
Samuel. David and his kingdom have sinned. They have taken a
census of themselves, and this is reckoned 'o be pride of the most
dangerous sort—heaven will not pardon our boastful statistics, and
the thunderbolt falls. David, sitting in his royal court, sees Gad the
seer coming in. We can only suppose that when the king saw Gad
among his morning callers, he prepared his mind for the worst.
Gad is the spokesman of heavenly vengeance, and he comes straight
to the point—he offeis David the choice of penalties: as the magistrate may do to you or me, one day—three months, with the option
of a fine. So David is given the option: seven years famine, three
months flight before the face of a victorious enemy, or three days of
mortal plague. What a frightful choice! Whatever David says, he
will be voting the death of many loving subjects; he may even be
voting his own. David can only think of one thing. Let God smite
us with his own hand, for then it must be somehow good in the
end, however awful it appears. If he punishes us by smiting our
crops, the consequences will drag themselves out inevitably through
agonies of famine. If he sets the Philistines or the Moabites on to
smite us, they will act on the impulse of their own cruel hearts, not
by the measure of God's justice. No, let God smite us by a direct
stroke, and let him smite us himself: let him pierce us with the
arrows of his pestilence. Then he will know when to stay his hand,
and we may even move him to pity by our prayers. Such was the
thought which flashed through David's mind. And he said to Gad
the seer, 'I am in a great strait; but it is better I fall into the hands
of the Lord—for his mercies are great—than that I fall into the
hands of man.' God respected his choice; the pestilence came, the
people died by thousands. David, like the good shepherd he was,
prepared to give his life for the flock. He stood in the path of the
angel of plague. 'I have sinned,' he said, 'and done amiss. These
poor sheep, what have *they* done? Turn thy hand against me, and

against my father's house.' God took the will for the deed; accepted a burnt offering from David, in place of his life; and called off the pestilence.

Evidently David's heart was sound; but his medical science was not. Infectious plagues are inflicted by microbes, just as military defeat (had David chosen that) might have been inflicted by Moabites. And if little was to be expected from the tender mercies of Moabites, still less was to be expected from the tender mercies of bacilli. If you and I agree with Gad the Seer, and accept the three days' pestilence as a divine judgement on Israel, we shall want to insist that, just as much as military disaster or failure of crops, it was inflicted by God through intermediate agents—in this case, through germs. And that is merely typical of the way God governs us. He controls our physical existence—yes, and our mental existence too— but he controls it as part and parcel of this mighty universe. He overrules, he directs. We are always in his hands, we never slip through his fingers. But being in the hands of God, we are in the hands of his creatures too. We never fall into the hands of God, and *not* of his creatures: never into the hands of God, and *not* of our fellow men: never under the action of God, and *not* of microbes, or of sunlight, of teaching, or of propaganda, of sympathy, or of hostility, or of some other forces belonging to this world, whether good or bad: never wholly, utterly or merely into the hands of God— never, except in one case. If we fall clean out of the world, if we die, then we fall into the hands of God alone. And that sounds alarming. And yet a man, threatened either with execution or (if he escapes that) with scientific brain-washing, might well pray to be executed, and borrow David's very words. 'I don't know what these men will do to me; and I don't know (come to that) what God will do to me, except that, whatever God does to me, will do me good at last. I am in a great strait; but let me fall into the hands of God (for his mercies are great). Let me not fall into the hands of men.'

King David, I take it, scarcely believed in immortality, or hoped for it. But by choosing to fall into the hands of God, because his mercies are great, he showed that he had in him the soul of religion, and the foundations of what was going to become our immortal hope. The idea of death—our being stripped of all bodily conditions, and taken out of the whole comforting, reliable system of created things—the idea is horrifying: it defeats imagination, it baffles even philosophy, for it takes us into a region where we stop being able

8

to think. Yet by this horrifying fate, and by no other, we fall into the hands of God, *not* of his creatures. We are placed at God's free disposal, for him to do with us according to his great mercies, and not according to the requirements of a vast physical system, this world God has created, and which he is, as it were, committed to uphold.

There are non-Christian theories of the after-life which sometimes charm Christian minds for a very bad reason—they make the other world seem comforting and familiar, by giving it the same sort of look as this world of ours, in which we are so much at home. This world, though God made it, is a sort of self-running system, going by fixed laws; and according to Indian thought, or to the western theosophy which copies it, the invisible world is much the same. There are fixed laws of spiritual destiny, which govern the movement of our souls from one life into another. God, doubtless, is understood to stand behind, maintaining the system of souls; just as we believe him to stand behind, maintaining the system of bodies, of atoms, stars, and galaxies, the physical world in which we now live. So, according to the Indian doctrine, we do not, when we die, fall into the hands of the living God; we merely pass from one pigeon-hole to another, in the one vast self-running system which God directs. To escape from the system altogether is at the best a remote and pious hope, open, perhaps, to the wise and perfect, after a thousand lives and deaths. It is not something that happens to us, whoever we are, and whenever we die.

Now Jesus was wise and perfect, if ever man was: and yet (in the faith of the Bible) he did not have any privilege in the way he died. Just as we do, he dropped out of the world completely, he was stripped utterly bare, he fell into the hands of the living God. But at the touch of the divine life he was instantly reborn; his manhood became all that God could make it; he shone forth as a pure expression of heavenly glory, as the highest revelation of what God will do with the soul that falls into his hands, because his mercies are great.

God's mercies are great: and that is why heaven is heaven. It is, indeed, a fearful thing to fall into the hands of the living God: he burns us as fire (so impure we are) before he begins to shine on us as light. Yet it is the best that can be promised us, to fall into the hands of the Lord, because his mercies are great: eye has not seen, nor ear heard, neither has entered the heart of man what God has prepared for them that love him.

Our pictures of heaven are all of them false; they are mere copies of earthly ceremonies, and worldly joys. The everlasting choir of heavenly harps and voices does not seem so stupid to us, as it did to our grandfathers, because we are a music-loving generation; and some of us, for brief periods, can find in music a little heaven on earth. But however congenial it may be to our taste, the music of heaven is only a figure of speech for something else; something which eye has not seen, nor ear heard, but which God has prepared for those that love him.

But can we do any better than the conventional pictures, the palms and the harps, in describing the heavenly state? If we try, we shall fail: and yet we will try, and if what we say is no better, at least it will be different. What shall we say, then, of those who have fallen into the hands of the living God, and experienced all the greatness of his mercy? Must we not acknowledge first of all, as the greatest of their blessings, a direct, unclouded perception of God himself? Think of it—God's thought and will shines always on their head; God's life and power tingles in their veins; God's love never ceases to warm their hearts. How much of God's mind the blessed ones know, is a question which wise theologians have discussed. They will not be able to explore the whole vastness of God's thoughts, but that will not be because they will be barred out, or because God is in any way remote from them. They will explore his glorious mind, as we may explore the beautiful variety of a mountainous country. We cannot explore all of it, but we can go where we like. Sometimes, when we are talking to a new friend, we find ourselves perfectly happy in exploring his thoughts and memories, his experiences and ideas, his feelings and attitudes—a magic and inexhaustible country. Now think what it will be to walk at will through the ways of God's heart.

The second blessing which they have is the natural consequence of their possessing God—and this is the glory which overflows from him into them, enriching their life and being.

Their openness to God carries with it a natural response on their own part. They cannot feel the heart of God, and not themselves share his love for a thousand other happy creatures. They cannot feel his creative touch upon them without being constantly transformed by it from glory into glory. They cannot know the will of God, without performing it, in all the splendid works that he has designed for them to do.

First, then, they know God, and secondly, they live gloriously; and in the third place, they are united by mutual fellowship among themselves. Even in heaven, it is right to think, we shall keep a fellow-feeling for our own kind, shall love men more dearly than angels; shall not be able, even, to delight in God himself, without calling in our friends to share our delight, while we also delight in their delighting. We shall read one another's hearts, and have no need of those natural veils and cultivated reserves, which in this earthly life mask shame, disguise ill-nature, or cover emptiness.

It is strange how, when we imagine heaven, we think of it as something shadowy. We colour it with the tints of moonlight, sleep, and the faces of the dead. But there are no shadows there; there is the substance of joy, and the vitality of action. When we are there, and look back on earthly life, we shall not see it as a vigorous battle-field from which we have peacefully retired; we shall view it as an insubstantial dream, from which we have happily awoken.

Earth is only a dream, compared with heaven; but this present life is no dream to us, while we live it. Nor does the hope of heaven persuade us to neglect present opportunities. On the contrary: if it is good to fall into the hands of God at last, it cannot be bad to throw ourselves into his hands here, as far as we are able; and that is why the sacrifice of Jesus is wonderfully enacted upon our altars. Here, in our Eucharist, is Jesus throwing himself into the Father's hands; and we are here, to be thrown too. For we are parts of his body: he does not disown us.

THE ULTIMATE HOPE

*—preached in St Andrew's, Headington, on the morning of
22 December 1968*

A speaker who knows his job saves up his main point, but I'm going
to spill mine out straightaway. My precious truth is this: that
Christian hope is not one thing, but two. It works on two levels,
and they are equally vital. There's hope for this world; and there's
hope for a world beyond it. There's hope for this world so long as it
lasts, and so long as it's ours to play with. For our God is a God who
does nothing in vain. He has not put us here to waste our time, or to
suffer mere frustration; there's something to be done here for God's
glory, and for man's well-being. Certainly our faith does not promise
us that the world will last for ever, or—what comes to the same
thing from our point of view—that the human race will indefinitely
survive to enjoy this corner of it. We are promised no such thing:
we are promised that our world, while it lasts and while we last,
will remain the sphere of God's creating and redeeming work; and
that he will make us men his workmen. So in the short view, there's
always hope; hope that frustrated in one line, we can open up
another; hope that if we have to suffer, our very sufferings can help
the good cause; hope that though we've wasted our chances, we
may be forgiven, and allowed a fresh start. We have only to put
ourselves into God's hands, for hope to spring fresh out of the
present day, and reach forward and claim tomorrow.

So much for the short view. Now what about the long? As I
was saying; our religion, so far from promising mankind a perpetual
survival, talks to us about a fated end to human history; and scientific prediction seems to chime in with biblical prophecy: the earth
will not remain for ever warm enough to support human life, or any
life, indeed. And that would be that, were it not for a fantastic
ray of further hope kindled in our days by space travel. Let the
earth turn to ice, people say; our far-off descendants will board
their spaceships and sail off into the galaxies; they will colonise
some planet over there just ripe for human habitation. A fantastic

hope, I call it, because the nearest habitable planet, if there is one, is likely to be a million times as far away as the moon and travel as fast as we may we shall be old and indeed dead before we reach it.

But set these reasonable doubts aside; suppose, if you like, the human race goes on for ever, by switching in due course from star to star, and hopping hither or thither over the enormous field of space. On such a supposition, would not the human race be immortal? Yes, on that supposition the human race would be immortal, if there were any such person as the human race; only there isn't. There's no such person as the human race, nor any such a thing; there's just Tom, Dick and Harry. Just Mary, Jane and Anne with all the other thousands of millions of individuals, dead, alive, or yet to be born. It is convenient to refer to the whole bunch of them as 'the human race'; but they, the individuals, alone are actual and the human race is a figure of speech, and a figure of speech is a queer sort of candidate for immortality. Tom, Dick and Harry are serious candidates for everlasting life; only in this world, and as physical animals, they just don't get it.

You may say, if you like, that human life goes on and on through history. But it's like a leaky pipe, running through sand, and fed at successive points with fresh injections of water. All along the pipe there's water in it: but all the water leaks out sooner or later to lose itself in the sand.

Such a leaky pipe is the history of mankind. As long as it lasts, there are men alive; but all the life of them leaks out and is (physically speaking) lost. Nothing and nobody runs on through the impressive panorama which historians study, or which seers venture to predict.

People say it is selfish to hope for immortal being, but it isn't because we are all in the same boat. If I'm a selfish man, I may hate the thought of my extinction. If I'm a loving man, I may hate the thought of yours. And if I'm a thoughtful man, I may hate, I must hate, the perpetual wastage of souls; of these precious products, the fine flowers of the world's growth, every one withering and fallen before it is perfect; or even if it touches some perfection, displaying its beauty for so brief an hour. And how can I be said to believe in God, if I think he has no remedy for this last frustration of his creative purpose?

But thank God (and here I return to my starting point) a Christian believer has two levels of hope. There's hope on the short view,

hope within the world, that something can be made of it. But beyond
that there's hope in the long view; hope that what we do in this
world is not all going to leak out of the pipe of history into the
sands of oblivion. So there are two levels of hope: and how stupid,
how perverse it is to set them against one another: to say, 'Well,
you must make up your mind; either fix your hope on this world, or
fix it on a world to come. If you fix your hope on heaven, you'll not
care a pin about the world's future; if you care about the world's
future, you won't give a straw for heavenly bliss.' Nonsense: we are
confronted with no such choice. Heaven alone gives final meaning
to any earthly hopes; and to take it the other way round, we have
no way to grasp at heavenly hope, than by pursuing hopeful tasks
here below.

It's extraordinary, the power people have for shutting their eyes
at what they don't want to see; there seems to be no limit to our
capacity for putting on blinkers: and men, serious worthy men too,
can go on concerning themselves with the progress of mankind, the
forward march of history, while blinding themselves to the fact that
there's no such being as mankind, nor any such a thing as history:
but that, from the historian's point of view, the wastage of men is
continuous, absolute, and final. People die off unblessed, but never
mind—fix your hopes on the next generation, or the generation
after that, and be careful not to notice that all those people in their
turn will die off disappointed, incomplete, and old. This leap-
frogging hope is fools' paradise; this is the delusive hope for ever
unrealised, of which it is said:

Hope springs eternal in the human breast:
Man never *is*, but always *to be*, blest:

Achievement perpetually elusive, spilt at last over the precipice of
death. The paradise of fools. But there is another paradise, and
waters welling up to everlasting life: waters bright as crystal (says
St John in his vision) springing out of the House of God and of the
Lamb; and on this side of the river and on that, an orchard of the
tree of life, every month yielding its fruit; and the leaves of the tree
for the healing of the nations, so that there shall be no more curse.
The throne of God and of the Lamb shall be there and his servants
shall serve him; they shall see his face, and his name shall be on
their foreheads.

I threw away my pearl of doctrine in my first sentence. Now let me see if I can get a second wind and a fresh start by throwing out a paradox, a sort of riddle, like this: The achievable cannot be achieved; only the unrealisable will ever be realised. 'Give me', says commonsense, 'a manageable assignment and I'll cover it.' Well, to a don like me it looks a manageable assignment to write a satisfactory book. But the writer is never satisfied with what he has written and it's out of date before the ink is dry. It seems a manageable assignment for any citizen to get his family a position of tolerable security and a pattern of family life which will yield contentment. But the ideal balance cannot be held: care and friction invade the house; time washes away the foundations.

That which is achievable cannot be achieved; only the unrealisable will ever be realised. The unrealisable: for example, to know God and to love him. Can I catch infinite God in my little net? Plainly not. Before I even begin, the project is seen to be beyond realisation. All these years I am supposed to have been learning to pray: that is, learning to join my mind with the infinite mind. And what happens when I pray? What will ever happen? Often the most a Christian can do is to put himself in God's presence: to make a mere act of blind, dry will in favour of God's purposes. If ever it seems to us that God lets a crack of light into our praying mind, can we attend to it beyond a moment? Can we walk all day in the beam of uncreated light? Or again, a Christian studies all his days to love his neighbour for God's sake. And what happens? What ever will happen? When shall you and I intercede for our friends as eagerly as we dream our selfish dreams? When serve any single person with the zeal with which we serve ourselves?

Such projects are unrealisable: and why? I have already said it: it is because I am trying to take eternity on board my narrow, perishable boat. Because it's eternity I'm trying to take on board, the project is unrealisable. But again, it's only because what I try to take on board is eternal, that there is any hope of realisation. My narrow hold will not contain immortal life; but no other goods I can stow there will stand the voyage: they will leak out and perish; God alone endures.

The greatest of German philosophers said that if man's spiritual quest is not to be a mirage (and in practice we can't think it is) then we must have infinite time in a future life to achieve our unachievable task, and overtake perfection. Ah, but the perfection we seek is not the rounding-off of ourselves, each of us a little god in our little blue heaven. Our perfection lies in God himself, whom not in ten thousand years, not in ten thousand thousand ages, not in time without end, can we reach or overtake. But he, in a moment, in the twinkling of an eye, can from his side break the deadlock, by linking us to himself.

> Then long Eternity shall greet our bliss
> With an individual kiss;
> And Joy shall overtake us as a flood,
> When every thing that is sincerely good
> And perfectly divine,
> With Truth and Peace, and Love shall ever shine
> About the supreme Throne
> Of him, t' whose happy-making sight alone,
> When once our heav'nly-guided soul shall clime,
> Then all this Earthy grossness quit,
> Attir'd with Stars, we shall for ever sit,
> Triumphing over Death, and Chance, and thee O Time.

Milton put these superb lines on a clock-case. He put them there to humiliate time, to put time in proportion: time, whose cruel creeping finger shows us how the hours pass and leave our projects incomplete, our days shortened. There is the clock, ticking away our earthly existence. How many minutes by the clock do our niggardly hearts give up to the adoration of the God who is the crown and the fulfilment of our being? No doubt John Milton, like the rest of us, might reflect with shame how slowly and how dully the moments all too often passed which he spared for looking his everlasting happiness in the face. Did he find comfort at such times in the lines he had written? If he did, let's hope it was not the comfort of mere compensation—not merely that the promise of eternal bliss hereafter made up for the present poverty of his praying hours. A genuine faith knows better. The eyes of God do not look at us out of an unimaginably distant future, they look at us from the heart of the present moment. He gives himself now and with both his hands. We try to pray. We hold ourselves before him while flat minutes pass, the effort on our side is cold and ineffective. But on his side there is infinite good pleasure. The touch of our spirit on his, little as we realise it, touches the pulse of everlasting bliss. When we awake to

God at last, we shall awake to the same eyes, and no other, as the eyes which look into our eyes now. There is only one God, and he is whole and entire in all his acts and ways.

Our knowledge of God now is the promise and the foretaste of heaven: apart from this present knowledge of God, we should have no clue to what heaven will be; for heaven is God. But it's just as true the other way about—without the heavenly promises God has given us, we should have no understanding of our present life with God. How could we make sense of the journey if we didn't know where the road leads? Unless the promise of heaven was shown us, how should we guess that the fitful gleams of spiritual light which visit us here flowed out from the steady and irresistible dawning of eternal day?

Compared with the sight of God in heaven our present glimpses of him seem little, or nothing, indeed: and yet they are not altogether nothing. Even today, when we pray, the hand of God does somewhat put aside that accursed looking-glass, which each of us holds before him, and which shows each of us our own face. Only the day of judgement will strike the glass for ever from our hands, and leave us nowhere reflected but in the pupils of the eyes of God. And then we shall be cured of our self love, and shall love, without even the power of turning from it, the face that is lovely in itself, the face of God: and passing from the great Begetter to what is begotten by him, we shall see his likeness in his creatures, in angels and in blessed saints: returning at long last the love that has been lavished on us, and reflecting back the light with which we have been illuminated. To that blessed consummation, therefore may he lead all those for whom we pray, he who is love himself, who came to us at Bethlehem, and took us by the hand.

A CHRISTIAN'S DILEMMAS

(1) SUBMISSION TO GOD OR MASTERY OF NATURE

—preached in Keble College Chapel, 1966

The plague broke out at Constantinople. The Christian Emperor consulted the Christian Patriarch and they ordained ceremonies of expiation and of national repentance to avert God's punishment. In saying that the people deserved the divine wrath, the clergy were, of course, on safe ground. The people always do deserve it. No observation can be more safely ventured in any age, than the observation that there is a lot too much wickedness about. But there was a physician in the imperial city who aimed at greater precision of diagnosis. The particular wickedness, he suggested, by which the men of Stanbul had attracted the divine wrath was neglecting the drains: and since it is hypocrisy to confess faults we do nothing to mend, sanitary measures might be more pleasing to God than litanies. Such was the physician's suggestion. Did they agree with him? No, they put him in irons for his impiety. The shafts of plague are the arrows of God. Shall we hope to avert his judgements by cutting his bowstring, or by blunting his darts? No, we must fall on our faces and pray.

The anecdote (which, by the way, is substantially true) puts the matter in a nutshell, and shows that the dilemma which forms my subject is by no means an artificial one. What practical meaning can attach to religion, if it does not teach us to accept the will of God? And once we have got it into our heads that this or that dispensation is the will of God, how are we to set about altering it by our own endeavours, as though it were subject to *our* will, not to his? It was on this point that Karl Marx laid so much emphasis. Religion teaches submission, and what could be more convenient to the exploiting classes? Marx would have liked to say that Christianity was an invention of the bosses for keeping the masses down: only he knew too much history to say it. Christianity was then, not so much the device of tyranny, as the expression of servility. Slaves lacking the power or the spirit to revolt conceived a religion, which patted them on the back for hugging their chains.

Was Marx right? He was certainly not plain wrong. Religion as a human phenomenon, like everything human, is good, bad, and indifferent. There has been plenty of bad religion. Religion, as men have conceived of it, has been useful to princes, and consoling to serfs. And superstition, time and again, has paralysed practical action: it has multiplied litanies, and neglected drains.

The modern world has turned its back on all this. If we are godless, it is not out of mere pride, selfishness or unspirituality. It is from a practical conviction that there is no rule, but the common good: and no god, but the human will. Admittedly the world is unimaginably vast and largely intractable. But whatever is to be done, we must do: and we have no one to wait for, but for one another. So let's get on with it. Let's plan politics for peace and prosperity; let's harness nature to our safety and enjoyment. An endless task, no doubt, but so much the better. An unlimited prospect, an open hope, an exhilarating aspiration: who can tell where man will stand in a thousand years? In a hundred, for that matter: or, indeed, in fifty?

It must be obvious to you that the substance of this godless view is shared by modern Christians—this godless view, if godless it is. For that is just the point we have to consider. And what are we to say? Is our religion an embracing of God's will? Yes. Does our religion identify God's will with the existing set-up either in nature or in society? Emphatically *no*. Christ came to transform the world, not to conform to it; and the transformation was to be physical as well as moral. It was, of course, useless for Christ or his Apostles to tell their humble contemporaries to set about transforming their physical environment. They had neither the knowledge nor the means. But Christ and his Apostles declared it to be the will of God that the physical world should be transformed—transformed in such a way, as to become the proper habitation and the obedient servant of the spirit. They saw the great change as coming about through some mysterious act of God, which should first shatter the existing order and then renew it.

The author of the Epistle to the Hebrews takes his stand on the principle, that man has been appointed king of the world as viceroy to God: and that all things must be put under his feet. He preaches from the text in which the psalmist says to his God, 'What is man, that thou art mindful of him, or the son of man that thou visitest him? Thou hast made him a little lower than the angels: thou hast subjected all things under his feet . . .' The writer to the Hebrews goes on to object that the prophecy is unfulfilled; all things are not subject to the dominion of man. Never mind, he says, they are destined to be so: Mankind, redeemed in Christ, will be the master of the world to come.

Now here we have two prophecies about man's destiny as master in the house of nature: the old Christian prophecy, and the current secular prediction. They point broadly in the same direction: but they are based on different sorts of evidence. The evidence for the current secular prediction is well known; it is the mounting success of technological science. Since we have done so much, we are confident of doing far more. The evidence for the old Christian prophecy was not any plain empirical fact like this. It was the profound conviction that man, uniquely cast in the image of God, was called to vindicate his maker's glory by mastering all inferior things. The grounds of the two prophecies, then, are certainly different, but they do not stand in any kind of conflict or opposition. Man's power to reason, to understand, and to invent are certainly among those godlike powers which show us to be made in God's own image: the good Apostles, if they visited (and perhaps they do visit) this world of ours, would agree, surely, that it is by our godlike capacities we have triumphed so far as we have over the stubbornness of nature.

Would they say, then, that the movements of material progress now afoot would if realised sufficiently fulfil the hopes with which Christ had inspired his followers then? They would not: they would say that scientific penetration and technical contrivance, though true parts of the divine image in man, were secondary parts of it. The divine image had been branded in their minds by Christ alive, dead, and risen: and Christ was neither a scientist nor an advanced technician: he was a village carpenter, and he was incarnate love. For God was in his flesh. The calling and destiny of mankind is not primarily to rule the lower world: it is primarily to be divinised; to be adopted into union with God, and made one with his heart; and *therefore* to rule with and under God the world which God rules.

Christianity has constantly been digesting new historical situations; there's nothing special in that regard about our own era. The two snakes, Christianity and modernity, are out to see which can swallow which. Faced by such an issue, we are driven back to a scrutiny of our origin in Christ and in the Apostolic Faith. Again and again we discover that the more true we are to our old title-deeds, the better able we are to meet our present liabilities. And so it is in the immediate case. The Gospel which proclaims the triumph of God's image in man can swallow very happily the secular hopes of our time, and assign them their place in a comprehensive faith, which looks for the manifestation of God's glory, the putting of all things under the feet of the Son of Man. The task of our Christianity is to see to it that man shall be truly human, that is, that Christ should have him: for none can be truly human, without being made partaker of the divine.

From so high and splendid a thought we had better descend in conclusion to the practical level. What after all are we to say about a Christian acceptance of God's will? Let us say this. God's will is expressed in two ways: in facts and in leadings. Facts express God's will in the sense that they set us our tasks: and the task is very often that we should alter the facts: our sins, for example, or our neigh-bour's unhappiness. Nothing forces God's will on me more plainly than your unhappiness or than my sin. There is seldom good reason to accept facts as divine dispensations under which we must simply submit. When it comes to dealing with the facts, we look for divine leadings: we have the words and example of Christ, and of his saints; we have our prayers, by which we seek to touch the living move-ments of God's present creative work. For he is at work in us indi-vidually, and in our neighbours singly, just as he is in the great movements of mankind. And it is men after all, it is the souls he makes immortal, that God supremely loves. What shall it profit men to master the universe, if they have hollow hearts? What shall it profit a man to gain the whole world, and lose his own soul?

A CHRISTIAN'S DILEMMAS

(2) PIETY OR HAPPINESS

—preached in Keble College Chapel, 1966

I feel myself unlucky to be preaching the last sermon in this series of Christian Dilemmas, for by now, surely, you must have seen the trick of it . . . Of course, you say, he's going to begin by pretending there's a dilemma, and then go on to show there's no dilemma at all. Very well then: I give in. Piety *or* happiness? Nonsense. We should enjoy our religion.

Enjoy our religion. I can hardly pronounce the words without a cold shiver running down my spine. I feel the eye upon me—the wicked eye of one of those smooth young professionals who interview unlucky Christians on the air, or on the screen. 'With all due respect, Doctor,' he says, 'I am surprised to hear you admit anything like that. Isn't it just what the critics of your faith say, that religion is an enjoyment, an indulgence in agreeable feelings and comforting ideas, with which believers soothe themselves? No doubt that sort of thing has its psychological value in certain cases, but is not it more important for people in general to be aware of the appalling facts of our human condition? While there are millions starving in Africa,' etc., etc. Whereas, of course, if I'd taken the other line, the interviewer wouldn't have been any better pleased. 'No,' I say: 'religion confronts us with the holy will of God: and the effect is not pleasant at all. It is deeply mortifying.'—'I realise, Doctor,' he rejoins, 'that what you say is extremely orthodox, but I confess I was hoping you'd give us a fresh lead. To judge from prayers and hymns, there's always been a great deal of groaning about the impossibility men find of being divinely perfect: but doesn't all that tend to discourage us from tackling the vast problems of our human condition. While there are millions starving in Africa,' etc., etc.

As you can see, the young man's trouble is not that he wants tears, and I offer him smiles: nor that he wants smiles, while I offer him tears. His game is, he chooses to assume that religion is bogus; neither the smiles nor the tears are related to reality; and neither of them lead to any useful action.

We might begin, at least, by lumping the smiles and the tears together. No one really believes in impassivity. Great joys and sharp griefs are the healthy reaction of men who expose themselves to life, and open their hearts to their neighbours. The hero of an ancient and famous poem finds himself destitute in a strange city where strange men walk by with impassive faces. He comes to a new building where they are carving on walls—why yes, carving them with scenes from his war, the war of Troy, and carving with a sense both for sorrow and for splendour. They have just cut out the figure of his old king. He exclaims:

> And look,
> Priam! Even here glory her laurel wears:
> Here mortal fates are felt: things have their tears.

The truth is that grief and joy, like hunger and a full belly, have their alternate places in the rhythm of life, and the index of happiness is not found by weighing the proportion between them. The truest evidence of our judgement about happiness may be found by observing whom we most sincerely envy. How can I ever cease to envy that little aunt of mine, the slightest, the least robust of women, who from her youth to her seventieth year carried on her tiny shoulders a weight that might have crushed Atlas himself; the hospital and the whole medical service of a remote Indian town with all the district round it? Shall we pity her the sorrows of her compassion for an evil often too great to do more than touch, or the pains, the dangers of her own body? Shall we grudge her the joys of work achieved, of life saved, of grateful affection outpoured? We may doubt if we have either the virtue or the calling for such a life: but ah, if we had! If we have a calling that is worth pursuing, then so long as we pursue it, our happiness is entire: sorrows and joys can be left to look after themselves.

My little aunt exposed herself to the truth. She was certainly no philosopher, but she was clear on certain points. Christ had died for her, and he had died for the peasants of India no less. The community to which she belonged had missions in those parts, and they were short-handed. She had no need of any more truths than these. She had a call from the living Eternity, which over-arches us all; and she had a call from a pinpoint in the Indian map; and the two calls were one. They lasted her her life long. Her hospital did not; as the work grew she rebuilt it twice from her own designs. Her body scarcely did—she nearly died twice from blood poisoning, by operating under impossible conditions, where the proper anti-septic precautions were not available. She survived and her calling lasted her out her working days. She was a humble Christian. There have been more Christians like this than some of you realise.

When we converse in the chilly atmosphere of a B.B.C. studio we are driven to use polite euphemisms, and to talk about 'enjoying one's religion'. No decent Christian wants to talk like that; merely to accept such terms of language is to falsify the issue. What Christians talk about is 'finding one's joy in God'.

We did not see much prospect of joy of any kind, when the aeroplane which should have brought us from New York to London was found to be non-airworthy, and we were faced with a five-hours' delay; nor did we see much mitigation of misery in the second-hand book stall, stocked as it was with manuals of gadgetry, with old chestnuts, cheap thrillers, and bad smells. There was only one paperback I thought I could read, and that was St Theresa's *Interior Castle*: how it got there, goodness knows. And so, in sheer desperation, I found myself opening a spiritual classic. And there it all was, the old plain monastic virtue, set out in the homely phrases of that no-nonsense Spanish lady. It is the same theme essentially as Thomas à Kempis's *Imitation of Christ*; only the style is less biblical and more down-to-earth.

Do you read Thomas à Kempis? You might do a lot worse. You will be moved and awed, but also a bit perplexed. For Thomas and Theresa put the issue of life and death before you in an unfamiliar form. It's a choice between seeking your happiness—your consolation as they put it—in created things, or in God alone. And this sounds like a religion not for a monk, merely, but for a hermit. What is the use of your or my reading a book which forbids us to find our happiness in one another? Thomas à Kempis seems actually frightened of friendship: he is afraid of loving his neighbour better than his God. That, surely, is as unchristian as it is fantastic. What is the use of reading such a book any further? And yet—and yet Theresa and Thomas refuse to be thus set aside: as we read them, we cannot resist the urgency of their plea or the force of their rebuke.

9

May I tell you my recipe for dealing with these authors? It is to ignore the negative part of their teaching. Never mind the advice about turning away from our fellow creatures. Whoever it applies to, it doesn't apply to me. Let me stick to the positive. My soul must perish if I cannot find happiness—consolation as they call it—in the will of God. How long am I to go on saying: 'I suppose I must do God's will. What a bore! Never mind, I shall still have some time off to console myself with light reading, or games, or social pleasures.' I do not want to learn to do without relaxation: I want to learn to find a delight in the service of my creator. If I do, perhaps I shall need less relaxation: but that's a secondary point. The main thing is to delight in God and not to be a reluctant, slavish worker in his service. God's will is God himself: it is his love, for he is love. One thing at least I can do when I pray: I can remember that the duty God lays upon me is the means of union with his most glorious life.

If we look further into the writings of our old-time saints, we shall see that their achieved delight in God brought human happiness with it. Theresa's God-given duty is to govern her convent and direct her sisters: and of course she cares for them with all her heart; how could she do otherwise than share the care of God's heart for them? It is another case of 'Seek ye first the Kingdom of God, and all these things shall be added unto you.' Only Theresa has reached this position by a path of abnegation which few are called to follow. It will be enough for me, if I can find consolation in God, and not in creatures alone.

'Happiness or piety' is, certainly, an absurd dilemma. We all set our hearts on something, and there is our happiness: piety is the name for a life which sets the heart on God. Theresa is only developing the saying of Jesus. 'Where your treasure lies, there will your heart be also.' And what a treasure that heavenly treasure is! Once get the lid of that box open, and out flies a very different throng than flew out of Pandora's box: the angels of God's will, leading us through the paths of all good purposes, and so by way of our appointed quests back to our meeting place with God.

FIXING THE WAGES

—preached in Pusey House, Oxford, 1962

I will tell you a terrible thing about the dons. The fellows of a college, meeting in their common-room, can fix their own salary-scales. There are, of course, certain invisible restraints. We may dip in the till up to the wrists, but hardly up to the elbows. On these embarrassing occasions, the most curious arguments are commonly advanced. Someone is sure to say, for example, that unless we make ourselves as rich as redbrick professors, or as rich as senior civil servants, we are all bound to desert our college in pursuit of these more lucrative employments. I see the gills of the philosophy fellow reddening up: and presently he explodes. 'Are we really as mercenary,' he says, 'as we pretend to be? If I take a chair in a University elsewhere, I shall have £200 more. But what will the money buy? I shall lose my place in a unique society of fellow-philosophers, I shall lose the nicest pupils in the world, and the friendships I've been cultivating for a decade. Heavens, we've actually been paid in this place for doing what we like best. Is it worth an extra £200, to go and do what would certainly bore us?' But the Fellow in Economics is still unconvinced. 'It isn't what the money will buy,' he says, 'it's the status-symbol of one's income-bracket. No one is prepared to go on for ever being bracketed with . . .' We never hear who these horrible people are, whose income-bracket it is death to share, because our philosopher explodes again. 'You and your status-symbols,' he says. 'You're not really so worldly as that; you just think that the rest of us are. It's the economic outlook, I suppose.'

'Worldly', says the college chaplain to himself, sitting in a corner, and (of course) holding his tongue. 'Worldly! I thought that was a Christian word, and our philosopher's an atheist.' He may be an atheist, but he's a philosopher; and it doesn't take a Christian to see through worldliness of this kind. A man who lives to increase his bank balance, or to keep up with (and if possible eclipse) the Joneses, doesn't know the a.b.c. of the art of happiness: there are so many jollier things to do.

I might preach to you against worldliness—indeed I might: there is a monstrous deal of status-seeking, and social climbing in the undergraduate world; and of course there's a beat world, just as much as an establishment world, to do your climbing in: why, there's a religious world to climb in, too. I might preach against this sort of thing, but if I did, it would hardly be a Christian sermon. We do not need to be Christians before we can prefer apples and pears to Dead-Sea fruit. A Christian should not be a worldling: no: but then a Christian should not be a fool.

When we are faced with the serious Christian dilemma, 'In or out of the world?' we are not concerned with worldliness of the vulgar kind. Worldliness is simply a temptation, a temptation besetting enough, heaven knows; but we have the answer 'Depart: from me, Satan: the Lord thy God shalt thou worship, and him only serve.' But when Jesus, victorious in his temptations, had vanquished the world, the flesh, and the devil, and set out on his saving mission, in the worship and service of the Lord his God, then he gave us two opposite standards of behaviour, which it may puzzle us to reconcile. He withdrew from men: and he identified himself with men. Not with men's worldliness: that he consistently hated, for worldliness is essentially *in*human: he identified himself with men in their warm humanity. When he dined with the rich publican, he was no moral skeleton at the feast of flesh. When he went to the Cana wedding, he doubled their allowance of wine; a gluttonous man, they said, a drunkard, a friend of taxfarmers and sinners. He wept with the mourners because they were sad, though the death of the body be no lasting evil; he restored Lazarus to his friends, because they longed to be reunited, though the general plan of nature, and the good purpose of God, lead the dead onwards, and do not turn them back. He gave his heart to the people: was it not for this reason that he was born a common man, and had a common upbringing? Had Herod's government been as liberal as ours I suppose he would not have taken a grant, or seen the University.

All this on the one side. But on the other side, he detached himself; threw off the ties of flesh and blood; shunned the crowds that pursued him; would not be the general healer of their common ailments; taught his disciples a mysterious love the vulgar could not understand; in the hour of his greatest need, prayed at a stone's throw from his closest friends; was resolved to suffer alone, and died uplifted in the air.

Modern readers are not the first to notice the paradox: the writer to the Hebrews had seized it. It behoved him in all things to be made like unto his brethren, that he might be a merciful and faithful high priest . . . for in that he himself hath suffered being tempted, he is able to succour them that are tempted . . . and much more to the same effect. But then on the other side: Such a high priest befitted us, holy, guileless, undefiled, separated from sinners, and lifted above the heavens . . . So what is the Christian to do, in imitation of such a Christ? Detach yourself from the world, live in the spirit, despise the creatures, seek the company of the saints, say some advisers. Nonsense, say others, monkery and mediaevalism! Be a man among men: identify yourself, especially with the least pretending.

> Play the pools and view the telly
> Swill the beer and aim the dart
> Starve the head and feed the belly
> Share the warm unthinking heart.

You may say I'm mocking: but the problem is perfectly real. Many of you would say of yourselves in moments of discouragement, that your religion cuts you off effectively from the body of mankind, without bringing you noticeably nearer to the life of God: while others, told to identify themselves with the masses, wonder whether the best method of realising their aim is not to be of no religion at all.

If we want to understand our puzzle, I'm afraid there is nothing for it, but to go to God himself. God, truly, is the abyss of wonder, and height of mystery: and yet there are truths about God that are clearer than the day. Is God removed from his creatures? Yes, by an infinite difference: he is God alone, and none of them is he. He is holy, uncontaminated: nothing beside himself enters into him, or forms the least detail of his life: no creature crosses the boundary that separates it from its creator. But then on the other side. Does God withhold himself from his creatures? Why, no, or how should they exist? Can we draw a breath, can we move a finger, without the will of God? He gives entire attention to each one of us. He knows my effort to speak of him, why, in this moment, he knows how much and how little it is worth in the throat and lips of a careless man. Your listening also he knows, how glad you are to think of him, how open to his good spirit.

Is it a paradox, then, that God is utterly separate in being and entirely present in love? It is not. If God were identified with any creature, or sunk in the being of the world, how should he be free to apply himself wholly and infinitely to every part of his universe?

Now if the Christian goes out of the world, where is he to go? If we make ourselves a little kingdom of the mind, and reign there we are still in the world, for our mind is a piece of the world and our thoughts earthly. If we make a little circle of like-minded believers, and live in it a life of our choosing, where are we, if not cut off in a corner of the world? We cannot get out of the world, unless we go into God, for everything is world, that is not he. And if we go into God, if he takes us into himself, it cannot be by union of substance—we cannot become parts of God—it can only be by union of will—he can attach our hearts to his. And what is his will? It is that free radiation of kindness, that compassion for evil and delight in good, which fills and warms all beings: it is the sunshine of the world.

We cannot be either detached, or devoted, as God is: not so detached, for are not we tied in a mortal body, one piece and fragment of the world? Nor so devoted to others, for we have not an infinite heart for them, but a heart limited to a few concerns, and then to one only at a time: a heart that forgets, that sleeps, that wanders; that tires, and drains dry as a cork. Yet we can detach ourselves from the objects of our appetites (that may be hard) and the objects of our hobbies or ambitions (that may be harder) by enslaving ourselves to the love of all the good that we can see. We cannot see a thousandth part of the good that God sees. Yet whatever good we do see, we shall see through the eyes of God: and his will be whatever care we conceive for the good that we can see, or compassion for the evil.

It is a pernicious snare, and a dangerous delusion, to think that we can unite ourselves with the will of God, by knowing better than our neighbours what God wills for them—except in the very broadest way. He wills their happiness, indeed; he wills their salvation. But if we think we are in the special secret of Providence, that we can be wise for others with the wisdom of God, we shall see our neighbours in the cold colours of our poor delusion, not in the rich truth of their actual being. We shall see a blueprint for their future, which we have presumptuously made, and not the present fact of their existence, which God has made. And if they sense what we

are at, they will also bitterly resent it. No: if we are to share the will
of God, it must be in the form of love. We must look first with his
eyes, then care with his heart. We must pray that steady contemplation may stir up pure affection. We must go out of the world into
God, but only that we may stand out of our own light, and see
things in the clearness of that uncreated beam, which is both the
truth of the world, and the joy of heaven, Jesus Christ our Lord.

FOR A MARRIAGE

*—preached in St John's, Westminster, at the wedding
of David and Valerie Morris, 10 September, 1966*

What is a preacher to do at a wedding? What can a preacher do at
any time? Perhaps you expect him to remind you of your duty, or
to help you bear your sorrows. But people coming to be married
have no sorrows—they are full of delight and we all share their joy.
They have a duty, certainly, but not a duty which they need any
urging to perform; their hearts are already set upon it. So what is the
use of a preacher? Yet a Christian preacher sets forth the mind of
Christ; and Christ, as you have been hearing, attended a wedding.
What, then, was Christ's concern—what is Christ's concern—in
the weddings of his friends? We do not read that he laid down the
law to them at that time, or told them their obligations—we read
that he concerned himself with the supply of their wine. It seemed
a shame to him, if anything was lacking that could spread abroad
delight. The bride and bridegroom drank from the cup. They
passed it round, and their friends tasted the very flavour of their joy.
Christ would not bear to see the flow of happiness interrupted, for
lack of wine in which to drink it.

Does this surprise you? Did you not expect Jesus to be the servant of natural delight, the abettor of warm-hearted pleasure? But
have you forgotten what Christ is? He is the desire of nations, he is
the joy of all mankind: he came to take away the cold religion of
duty, and to substitute the religion of delight. We are to do our
duty—yes, but we are to delight in it, for the love of our neighbour,
and for the dear love of God. There is nothing else but this, that we
can hope for in heaven itself—nothing but to do good unalloyed by
any meanness, and to do it with infinite delight. And how shall we
be able to do so? By feasting on the vision of a face, whose eyes are
the deep wells of happiness and love.

It is not surprising at all, then, that Christ should begin his
ministry at a wedding: for a true marriage is a special favour of
God's grace, and a direct foretaste of heaven. God's glory is

reflected, for those who truly love, in one another's faces; they see the Creator shining through his handiwork, and the vision inspires them with a simple delight in doing one another good, and in furthering God's will. Those who are being married know what they want to do: and it is exactly what God desires them to do. They do not, as the rest of us so often must, make themselves care about the will of God: they do care for it: for they care for one another.

I am not telling you that all weddings are wonderful or that there are no selfish couples, when each is out for what they can get. There are plenty such, but those are not Christian marriages. In a Christian marriage God inspires two people with an irresistible desire to join him in his own creative work—through them he is to create a new life-cell in the body of Christ—a newly shared existence, a newly founded home, a household, a family today, where yesterday there was none.

Well, but however genuine the marriage, the first enthusiasm, the inspiration of delight must fade. No, it need not merely fade. It will change its character, certainly. But Christian people, loving and married, have had a marvellous initiation into the religion of joy, they have had their eyes opened to the possibility of heavenly delight, they have seen that pleasure and duty can be one. It will be their own fault, if they ever lose the glory, or forget the lesson. Christ, in his first miracle at Cana of Galilee, not only multiplies the wine of happiness, he also brings it about that the best wine is kept to the last. You also have Christ at your wedding, and in your whole married life. You will not stop at the first stage: you will pray him who filled the flagons to open you the wellspring of perpetual joy and spread the happiness of your marriage through the whole extent of your lives. You who see the shine of God's handiwork in one another's eyes will learn to see it in a hundred faces: you who love God's will in the making of your marriage will live to love that will in the whole calling of your earthly life. The new miracle of Christ's religion is the union of duty with delight; but the miracle of miracles, and masterpiece of wonders, is the keeping of the best wine to the last; and even that last is not an end, for, says Christ at the Supper, 'I will drink it new with you in the Kingdom of God.'

3.

For Prayer

YOU WANT TO PRAY?

'I didn't want a lover yet, but I wanted to want one,' says St Augustine of himself in his teens. When he says this he is looking back after many years: and I suppose he is half aware of making a parable between things earthly and things divine. The teenage predicament which he describes did not last him many months, but all through his young manhood, as he is bound to confess, his spiritual immaturity continued: he didn't want God yet, but he wanted to want him: *nondum amabat, sed amare amabat*. Well now, it is no use talking about prayer to people who don't want to pray; but before you decide that that rule cuts you out, let me see whether you cannot say at least that you want to want to pray; what a thing it would be, if your heart went out with joy to meet your Maker! If any of you has to say *nondum amo* you can still say *amare amo* and that will do for a start. For God is gracious.

But now what can I tell you? In talking of prayer, we want above all to be realistic; so let us begin with the dead bottom of the subject, and take a ground on which we can all find our feet. To pray is to confront the will of God. Even if you thought that nothing came through from the other side; even if you thought that you had to make all the running yourself; you would still be doing something perfectly real and absolutely necessary, in bringing yourself face to face with the will of God. And sometimes, perhaps, if you are in doubt or despair about prayer, because you start with high hopes and cannot realise them, it might be a help to cut your losses, and be content with simply facing the will of God. It is no trifling thing, surely, to look God's will in the face, and square your will with it, so far as you can. If you had never heard that prayer could be more than this, wouldn't you want to do this, and to do it every day?

A serious atheist might say, 'But now you are simply talking of facing your duty. I can do that; I do it every morning.' Quite right: and what a blessing if he does. But poor man, he thinks of life in terms of duty: we know our lives in terms of God. God is not a prop

hitched on to the backside of duty, to hold it up. Duty is merely a
bad shorthand name for the mind of God concerning us; and a
Christian, on the deeper levels of thought or feeling, has nothing to
do with duty. His dealing is with God; and that is why he has the
secret of life, and the atheist lacks it. Admittedly we Christians are
practical atheists for too much of our time, and see life in terms of
duty, integrity, and moral pride; our idea of ourselves, or our
neighbours' idea of us. Just so: but since that is so, it is infinitely
worthwhile to pray, if only to realise that in all our life it is God's
will with which we have to do.

We start, then, with the point of contact: I have to face God.
From that point we can spread out in both directions: we want to
see to it that what is really I faces what is really God. What is really
I! The first thing to get straight here is that I am scarcely real at all.
Real enough in one sense, no doubt: look at all this skin and bone,
all this largely worthless activity, all this dreaming, all this emotion,
much of it bad. But what is that real I which has to meet God's will?
It is the willing I, the I who chooses and cares; and *what's* my will?
Which way does the current run? The lines of my will are like the
tangle of broken and crisscross lines in the palm of my hand, which
the clever palmist says she can read; and doubtless God can read
the chequered pattern of my unreality. But when I come to pray, I
do not come to have my morality deciphered: I come to be pulled
together into something more real, and something far more simple.

But if I am to be made more real, I must start from where I am,
and with what I am. The only self I can bring to God is the bundle
of my choices and desires. Sort the bundle out, and you have the
familiar branches of prayer all before you. For what are your
desires? They are good, bad, and indifferent. Those that are bad
you might have managed to forget (we are all very cunning at that),
if they hadn't made their power so plainly felt in yesterday's conduct: examine your life, and you seize them. Needless to say, of
bad desires you have nothing to do but to repent, and turn away
from them. Some of your desires are good: but they are not nearly
good enough, pure enough, strong enough. You have them out
before the face of God, and give them some exercise, and acknowledge, with awe, that they are parts of his holy will.

But a great body of your desires are indifferent, neither ignoble
nor noble. Do not leave them wholly out, when you come to God,
for they are most of you: but talk to God about the things that

really concern you, even though they are neither directly to be repented of, nor directly to be made into prayers: but let them find their place, and learn their true proportion, in relation to God's holy will. For he wants you to be a human animal, surely, to play and to enjoy and to realise yourself: only he does not want you to be either a playboy or a drone or an egotist. How do such matters come into our prayers? The natural and happy part of life is for most of us the chief field of thanksgiving to God. Joys we can sincerely give thanks for will not be selfish, nor disproportionate to other concerns.

I say, bring yourself before God, the self of choice, concern, desire. But I have not yet said the most important thing about it, which is this: that yourself, especially in the worthiest part of it, is largely made up of concerns for, and attachments to, other people. Praying for your fellows is not something different from bringing yourself before God: for your concerns for them are half your heart, and you would be a better man, if they were far more than half of it. When you come before God, fix your eyes on him and on those for whom you pray. The more you look outwards, the more you will be yourself. For love is the substance of character, and love self-forgetfulness.

But (I think you will say to me), I couldn't seriously pray for my friends if I thought I was merely exercising my kinder desires, by dwelling on their names with affection. I have to believe that it does them some good. Very well; but you *can* believe it. And now I'm going to surprise, and if possible, shock you. I'm going to talk about spiritualism. What can spiritualistic mediums do? Can they communicate with the departed? No, there is no evidence that they can. But there is so much evidence that it is silly to dispute it, of their receiving into their minds masses of material out of the hearts and memories of the living, with which they recreate the images of departed persons unknown to themselves by ordinary acquaintance. Now spiritualistic mediums are freaks: but they are not absolute freaks. It is very unscientific, indeed, to believe in absolute freaks anywhere in nature. Freaks are special developments of common characteristics. Mind does everywhere flow into mind. How it happens is neither here nor there: it happens. Spiritualism teaches its votaries to make a forced and abnormal use of this power, a use leading to illusion. True religion teaches us the true use of it; and that use is nothing else but intercession. We place our hearts at the disposal of God's will, to spread that influence which he has placed in us in support of our friends' happiness or virtue. We don't have to think a lot of ourselves, or of our spiritual powers, to do that; for influence will flow from us in any case; only, if it is not submitted to God's direction it will be as likely to be bad as good, depressing as uplifting.

I began by saying that prayer would be a great thing, even if we thought nothing came through from the divine side. But you see that in fact you can't believe this blighting negative. As long as your prayers are about yourself, perhaps you can keep it up: *you* repent, *you* face God's demands, *you* resolve, *you* aspire. But when it comes to intercession, it just won't do. Am I to bless my friends? No, God shall bless them, and he shall bless them through my prayers; my little wishes shall become the instruments of his omnipotence. And why not? When I resolve and aspire on my *own* behalf, there is much impurity and darkness in my mind, much adulteration of self-regard in my best endeavours. But when, in the sight of God, you wish well to another, can even the Spirit of God himself get a knife's edge between your wish and his own will? For God is love, and he that abides in charity abides in God.

But when we have seen that God comes through into our prayers for our neighbours, we shall not be able any longer to keep him out anywhere: so, after all, let us pray, with faith that we shall be inspired, for God is in the ground of our hearts.

I must make an end, though I have still said nothing of what may be most important—how we should realise the presence of God and so adore him.

But it really doesn't matter. I meant this to be a useful sermon. But nothing one says from the pulpit on this subject is any great use at all. Only one thing is of use: and that is individual consultation. Are you satisfied with your prayers? Why don't you ask for advice? What can be more natural than to say to a clergyman, may I make a date to come and talk to you about prayers?

Jesus taught his disciples to pray, and his ministry in this regard remains alive in the Church, so long as the Church lives. We must let our Christian friends and Christian pastors help us, that we may worthily perform the first duty of a rational creation, and worship with our heart the Maker and redeemer of our souls.

GRACE AND RESURRECTION

—preached in Mercers' Chapel, London, Lent 1963

Last week, when we had given a party, I admired the politeness of
our guests, who, occupied as they might be, found time to write us
an acknowledgement next morning. So it occurs to me that it is
time I thanked the Worshipful Company for the dinner they gave
me forty years ago, and which, graceless youth that I was, I never
acknowledged in such a manner. That was the last time I was at
Mercers' Hall, and the only time previous to this that I had the
honour of addressing the Worshipful Company. I still have the
dress coat which I got made for the occasion; the moths have had
their meal of it, but still I have no other. This I do remember, you
gave the very kindest hearing to a boy speaking on behalf of St Paul's
scholars; and you will need to be just as indulgent to a man who
speaks to you on behalf of your Creator. For I do not need to tell
you that all preaching is folly: no one can speak worthily of divine
themes. Those who judge a sermon, will always find plenty to
criticise; those who listen for divine wisdom, may receive hints of it
even from the mouth of a man so unwise as to the claim that he
speaks in the name of the Father, and of the Son, and of the Holy Ghost.

I will take as my subject, the power of God. Let me explain what
I mean by such a title. I do not propose to roll you out sounding
sentences on the almightiness of the creator's will, that will apart
from which there would *be* no world at all; apart from which I should
have no voice to address you, and you would have no ears to hear
me; for neither you, nor I, nor anything would have any being, but
for the will and the power of God. A fine subject, no doubt, to
preach upon; but not, perhaps, a very practical one. The practical
question about the power of God is this; what can we look to him
for? If we trust him, what do we trust him to do? No doubt it is
very pious, and very proper, to say, that the whole system of nature
expresses God's creative will; and that the more we discover about
nature's laws, the more reason we have to admire both the consistency and the intricacy of God's ways. That's all very fine; the God

of nature can be worshipped, in a dumb and distant sort of way; but
how can he be prayed to? And how can he be trusted? If we pray to
him, what can we ask him to do? And if we trust him, what can we
trust him to perform? Is not he committed by his own consistency
to the rules of the system he has created? How can we ask him to
act out of order, that he may answer our prayers? How can we rely
on him to save our children from disaster, if the disaster is coming
to them?

When we pose the practical problem about the power of God, we
are not questioning his almightiness. He need not have made this
world: he made it: nothing resists his will. But, in view of his com-
mitment (so to speak) to the world-order, what can he wish to do
for us, except to let us be swept along in the great process of nature?
Suppose a musical composer were conducting his own newly
written symphony: and suppose the little man who does the drums
were suddenly to put up his hand, and ask to have the score altered
—he hadn't a sufficiently interesting part. What could the composer
do, but explain to him the structure of the piece? And what answer
can our prayers or wishes discover, other than this—to be told to
study the way the world goes, and why?

There is the problem, and of course it's extremely familiar: you
are already wondering why I should waste so many words in expounding the obvious. Don't we all know that this is where science
has got faith into a corner? Yes, no doubt. But there's an odd fact
about the scientific position. We think that the success of our great
scientific enterprise has tied the hands of God, by committing him
to his own laws. Yet in tying (as we think) the hands of the Almighty
we have been freeing our own. In one sense, this is obvious; everyone recognises that a knowledge of nature's laws is a mastery of
nature; our knowledge sets us free to do, within limits, what we
choose, even if it is to fly to the moon. But not only does science set
man free from a thousand age-old shackles; science is also itself a
vast enterprise of man's free initiative. The laws of nature do not
disclose themselves; they yield their secret to the free endeavours of
investigators; to clearly thought-out soundings, and to cleverly
thought-up hypotheses. Science is the work of wit, and wit is ours,
wit is free.

So here is the puzzle, here is the paradox; the further we explore
the law-bound regularity of things, the more we experience the free
power of exploration. We, the explorers, are free, however tied up

the forces of nature may be. And what are we? We are certainly parts of the world, whatever else we are besides; and if God made the world, he made us, too. It would seem, then, that God cannot be tied down by the pattern of a world-plan he has himself adopted; for look, he made us, and in some of our doings we are as free as air. So God's plans must allow for free operators, after all.

What is more, God's plans do not simply leave room for free operators, they employ free operators in carrying them out. The hand of God is most clearly seen in what is highest and best; that is, in the free flowering of the human spirit. We shall have the whole of religious insight against us, if we attribute the works of nature to God, and the works of the spirit to ourselves; what is more divine than the charm of character, the fire of genius, the steadfastness of virtue, the unselfishness of love? These things are not merely the masterpieces of God's hand, they are the sole revealers of his nature. No one can think that God is any sort of radiation, or of energy, or of physical structure; but if he is not some sort of wisdom, some sort of loving-kindness, some sort of free creating power, then I have no notion what he is, and even the mention of his name is sound without sense.

It is what man is, then, that most clearly shows the print of God; not, however, what man is by nature, but what man freely achieves. Serene wisdom, heroic charity, inventive cunning, these are the principal and most revealing works of God; but none of us has these glories by nature, they are achieved by choice, effort, and freewill.

I want to press upon you the whole force of the paradox, that what is most freely our own is most truly God's, what is most fully our achievement is most entirely God's creation. We make ourselves what we are; but God makes us make ourselves what we are. Men can make dolls and machines: God alone can create creators, yes, and create through their hands.

The highest piece of wisdom which the world knows on this subject is the Christian faith in Christ. The Christ of faith is not some figure remotely supernatural about whom ingenious doctrines have been propounded by theologians. He is the very heart of the present matter. For consider; what do we mean, when we call the man Jesus, Christ and Son of God? We mean that the action of Jesus was simply the action of God. But what was Jesus? Was he a divinely mesmerised sleepwalker, a jointed doll pulled by heavenly wires? Was he a painful pedant, carrying out with pharisaic exactitude a part which had been written for him by a divine hand? He was all the reverse of this. Never was there a man whose words and actions were more utterly his own. The spontaneity of his compassion moves us to tears. the blaze of his indignation shocks us: his speech is an unforced poetry, the coinage of his heart; the sacrifice on which he spent his blood was a decision personally made in agonies of sweat. If any man made his own life, Jesus did; yet what was the impression he left on his friends? That his whole life was the pure and simple act of God. What Jesus did was simply what God did to save us all.

Now what I am saying is that this belief is no extravagance of religious fantasy; it is the most serious established conviction of twenty centuries, that if the action of God is anywhere to be seen it is in the free, the human life of Jesus Christ. The more human it is, the more it is divine; the freer it is, the more it is the will of God.

When we try to think about the mystery of God we inevitably become the victims of our own imaginations. We think about God in pictures, or in figures of speech; and presently we find ourselves taking the figures for facts and the pictures for portraits. For instance, we find it natural to think of God as being above us; and this *above* is indeed expressive; it speaks of the height and glory of the Godhead, outsoaring our fullest reach of thought. But God is not literally above us, nor need the picture of height become a tyranny in our minds. From another point of view it is useful to think of God as beneath us, his life everywhere underlying us: we are rooted in him, he is at the ground of the heart, at the spring-point of our freewill: we draw our life out of him, as water out of a well; or, better still, we clear the channel of our mind, that the fountain of his goodness may freely rise.

Here, anyhow, is a way of thinking, or of picturing, which may help us to see the life of Jesus as both human and divine; the creative power of God came out in the spontaneity of his freewill. But this is not just something we have to gape at, and worship from a distance in the person of Jesus Christ: it is the model and pattern which we have to follow. The divine power underlies our being also; the wellspring of life is in the ground of our heart, even if the channel is blocked with mud. We pray; that is, we lay our heart upon the heart of God, we surrender our resistances; something of the divine care for our friends and for our own perfection becomes our care; we love a little what God greatly loves and resolve, though feebly, what he firmly wills. This is the grace of God, and everyone who has ever received it knows this: the grace of God does not remove our own initiative. Far from it. The man who receives the grace of God says: Now I am really myself; now I am caring about what I really care about; now I am making a genuine decision. The more it's God, the more it's I: and the more it's I, the more it's God. And it's no use telling us that such a state of affairs is contradictory or impossible. For that's the life of religion: everyone who has tested it knows it to be true.

Is not it about time that we turned back to our original question? I think it is. We asked where, in a world bound (as it seems to us) by natural law, we may trust the power of God to act for us? Well, we have got some sort of an answer. The power of God will act for us in making or inspiring our freewill. In the language of theology, God will give us his grace. If this is a miracle, it is a miracle which is repeated every day in the lives of humble Christians, who repent and throw themselves back upon the sources of life. God will give grace: and if to us, then of course to our friends, and to thousands for whom we are free to pray.

We can leave it to philosophers to puzzle out, if they can, how it is that the system of this law-bound universe allows for God's grace, and for our freewill. We do not know *how* it is so, but we know that it is so, and the knowledge of the fact is enough for plain men to go upon. And if we begin to doubt the evidence of divine grace our humdrum lives afford, then we look to the shining examples of heroic saints, and beyond them, to Jesus Christ himself. Christ's life is the proof that God's power is not bound by laws of physical functioning.

When we have seen that God acts thus for our salvation within the world, we become brave enough to believe that he will also act for our salvation beyond the world. Because Christ's disciples saw that Christ's life was the act of God, they were able to see his death as the act of God, and to see the completion of God's act in Christ's resurrection. I do not know how the life of Jesus, broken and destroyed by crucifixion, was restored. It was not, anyhow, an event contrary to nature; it was beyond and outside nature. Christ's resurrection was revealed within the world; it was no part of the world. And so with the resurrection which God has promised us. It is neither contrary to the natural order, nor in accordance with the natural order; it is clean beyond the natural order; it is a next stage after nature has run her course. The God who made us and all things can continue, renew and enrich our being in another sort of life if he chooses; and he chooses.

If nature cannot stand in the way of God's action within nature, still less can she stand in the way of God's action beyond nature: if God is able to give grace in this present world, he is able to give resurrection in a world to come. So we have two answers, not one answer, to our original question. What does God do for us, in spite of natural order? He gives grace: and he raises the dead. These are the two focal points of Christian faith, the two basic assurances; and if we had nothing else but these, we should have enough.

Yes, if we had nothing else. But this is not all we have. In posing the problem, we accepted for the sake of argument the suggestion that God is so committed to the laws of physical nature, that in the direction of physical events he has tied his own hands. There is no good reason, in fact, to believe that the grid of natural law is as rigid as this, or the mesh of physical necessity so close. The whole world is subject to the infinitely subtle leadings and persuasions of God's good Providence. There are many physical blessings for which it is perfectly reasonable to pray; for health, for deliverance from pestilence and famine. Only that such blessings are to be prayed for with submission, and under correction; we do not know whether it is in the good pleasure of God to grant them or not. But for grace, and for everlasting life the disciples of Jesus may pray with assurance; the generosity of God has placed these best of good things ready to our hands; we have only to want them with all our desire, and we can carry them away.

Grace and Resurrection are the best of good things: and why? They are a sharing in the life of God himself. By grace, he fills with the inflow of his Spirit the leaky narrow vessel of our heart; by Resurrection he makes that heart a lasting and a fit receptacle to catch the overflowing glory of his presence. There light spills evermore from the fountain of light and streams from soul to soul; the more they hold, the more they give away, and all are rich by what each one of them receives; and none keeps back the unforced voice of thanksgiving and joy, the praise most justly due to God in Trinity of persons, Father, Son, and Holy Ghost; to whom be ascribed all might, dominion, majesty, and power, henceforth and for ever.

A CHURCHMAN'S DUTY

—preached in St George's, Bloomsbury, 1956

John ii, 17. His disciples remembered that it was written,
THE ZEAL OF THINE HOUSE WILL DEVOUR ME

I remember once talking to a man who had written a successful play for the London stage. It seemed a miracle to me: I wanted to know how it was done. 'You can't *do* it,' he said, 'just like that. It comes together, somehow, between the writer and the actors: it's half what the author wants to say, and half what the actors feel they can put across. Put an actor in an armchair, and as likely as not he's a rotten critic of your play: all an actor can be trusted to do is to act. Give him the lines, and start him rehearsing; he'll try the words this way, he'll try them that way, until he gets them how they want to be said. But sometimes, after trying every way he can think of, the actor turns to the author, looking pretty miserable, and says: "I'm sorry, I can't say it. You must alter it." And (said my friend) if he's a decent actor, he's always right. There *was* something false about the lines, they weren't in character, they hit the wrong note, they wouldn't do at all!'

Reading the Bible in Church isn't play acting, the last thing we want is stage tricks here, but it presents some of the same difficulties. The reader, like the actor, wants to say the words as they need to be said, and sometimes he gets a mouthful which he doesn't know what to do with. If any of you had been reading this evening's lesson, which is the text of my sermon, and if you had the author (that is, St John) at your elbow, wouldn't you feel inclined to protest: You've given me an impossible task. I can't say these words right. How do I make Jesus Christ drive the market out with a whip of small-cord? It's not in character. My Jesus is all patience and compassion: how is he to flame with intolerance, to act with anger, to throw down the tables, to reach for the whip, to drive the cattle out? It is bad enough (you might say to St John) that you expect me to speak with the lips of Christ at all: to say words which, properly heard and felt, are to break down the heart of man and let God into the world. It is bad enough, that I have to say such things at all: it is altogether too bad, when they just won't say.

If you made your complaint to St John, would he change the lines for you? He would not. He is not writing a play, he is recording a fact, which the other evangelists also record. He won't change a syllable. Very well then, it's only fair he should help us with the interpretation. In what spirit does Christ act? Is he staging a protest against the doings in the Temple? No, that's too artificial: he cannot have planned it all, he cannot have resolved beforehand to register spontaneous indignation. But then, is he caught out, overtaken with anger, carried away from the kindness in which he meant to remain? That seems even less credible.

'The trouble with you,' St John might say, 'is flying off into theories. Stick to the words I have written, and say them just as they come. TAKE THESE THINGS HENCE. MAKE NOT MY FATHER'S HOUSE A HOUSE OF MERCHANDISE. Turn it over on your tongue. Does not it taste right?'—Why, yes, it tastes divinely right. It's just— LOYALTY. This is my Father's house; I am his son. I cannot stand by, and see him dishonoured. It must not go on a moment longer. Take all this stuff away. What, you won't? Then I will!

If you and I have not the same sort of loyalty towards our human fathers, or towards our friends, so much the worse for us: if we stand by and hear them ridiculed; still worse, if we join in, and add our contributions to the slander. It is extraordinary how we betray our friends, and how we expect them to stand up for us. Or (as we think in our conceited minds) it's not extraordinary at all: for we, of course, are superior persons, viewing mankind from a great height, and awarding our acquaintance praise and blame with poetic justice, or if not with justice, anyhow with such charm, that even malice ought to be forgiven us. Whereas if they presume to exercise their wit on us—well, it's a scandal, isn't it? Aren't they our friends?

In our better moments, all the same, we can shed tears of shame for our treason, and see that a grain of loyalty is worth a bushel of malicious wit, or non-malicious wit, at that. It is ignoble to dishonour our friends, and scarcely less ignoble to let others dishonour them. Here's a proverb for you: It is magnanimous to bear insult against ourselves, it is pusillanimous to bear insult against our friends. Jesus was magnanimous, he pardoned insult to himself. They struck him, they spat upon him, and he said not a word. They hammered through his hands, and he said, 'Forgive them, Father; they know not what they do.' They taunted him for hanging on the cross, but he did not reply. That was his magnanimity. But pusillanimous he was not: he did not tolerate insult against his Father, not for a moment. Here was a temple, administered in his Father's name: here the tribes of mankind were to be welcome to their Almighty King. But here, in the place where men of non-Jewish race should have made their devotions, the noise, the profanity of a market: here the priests of God making so much per cent on selling beasts for sacrifice: beasts on which, when they had been sacrificed, the same priests were to feed. Jesus plucked a whip. 'Take these things hence,' he said: 'Make not my Father's house a house of merchandise.'

He did it, and he died for it. And if you had asked him, was it politic? Mightn't it be mistaken for rebellion? Mightn't it take the bread out of dishonest (or even fairly honest) men's mouths? I do not think that any of these questions would have moved him. There are times when a good man does not deliberate long, or weigh remoter consequences. How could he go wrong, to vindicate the honour of his Father?

Jesus was pre-eminent in the virtue of Religion. Religion, properly so-called, is not the whole of our spiritual life: it is not faith, for example, nor is it obedience. Religion is a practical concern for the honour of God: it is in some ways the purest, the most unselfish part of human duty; it does not aim at human advantage, but gives honour where it is most due, and glorifies the King of Glory. If it were possible (which it certainly is not) for a man to know that he would surely die and be everlastingly damned tomorrow, he could not make a better use of today, than in glorifying God, for then, when his light was quenched in misery and darkness, it would at least have shone a moment, before it went out.

And you—you whom he has not damned, but predestined, and called, and justified, and made partakers of his glory in Christ Jesus—what will you do for the honour of God? It is my duty tonight to set before you the obligations of a Churchman: and this is the light in which I ask you, for the present, to view them: as the acts of religion, the claims of God's honour on our loyalty.

The Jesus who threw the traders out of the temple foretold that *that* temple would fall, so that one stone would not remain upon another. After it had fallen in fact, he came to St John on Patmos, and, in the vision of the Revelation, delivered judgement on the new temple which God had raised up in the place of the old. For the Gospel is everlasting. What Jesus does in the Gospel he always does: he still visits, and purifies, the temple. He stands in our midst; and what does he find? Not cattle here, but cobwebs: and by which is his Father more dishonoured? By corruption, profanity, and noise; or by neglect, emptiness and disobedience?

The new Temple is not wood or stone: like Jesus its foundation, it is alive. Hear what St Peter says: 'Coming to him, the living stone, ye also as living stones are built up into a spiritual house: for ye are a chosen race, a royal priesthood, a holy nation, a people of God's own possession, that ye may show forth the excellencies of him who hath called you out of darkness into his marvellous light.'

Why compare a mass of people to a temple? What is the sense of it? A temple is rigid, square, clear-cut, a visible block, bearing its purpose on its face, unmistakable for anything else: and unless it has these characters, it cannot witness to God. Pull the stones down and pour them back into the quarry; they may be excellent stones, they will not be a Church. And so with us, whom St Peter calls living stones. As a point of history, let me assure you of this: from the first moment of its foundation, the Church was hard, clear, visible, and firmly knit: nothing mossy about its edges. Its members professed one truth—they would not have risked death for religion, if they had not been convinced of the Gospel. They submitted their lives to the congregation, under the leadership of the ministers whom Christ's Apostles had given them: if they were judged to have given scandal by their disloyal lives, they accepted penances from the Church, they fasted and wore mourning until they were re-admitted to communion. They paid for the upkeep of the poor. They were present every Sunday at the Holy Sacrament: if they were absent, they were assumed to be sick: they were enquired after and the Holy Communion was carried to them. Their heathen friends divorced their wives if they were tired of them: the Christians did not. Their heathen friends could make money in any profitable line: the Christians were forbidden a whole list of dishonest or indecent occupations. Their heathen friends rose in the government service: not so the Christians, because of the idolatrous oaths and other ceremonies attaching to public office under Caesar. The lines were clear enough, sharp enough, and costly enough, which silhouetted the living temple of God against a heathen sky.

This was the Church which Christ's Apostles built for the honour of God, and if they did not know the mind of Christ, it is useless indeed for you to think you will ever know it. These were your masters and fathers in faith, whose prayers from heaven you invoke. And what are you? Church of England men: members of a body whose peculiar glory it is to combine the form with the Spirit: to say with the Churches of the Reformation, what Christ said to Nicodemus, You must be born again; and to keep with the Catholic Church the form of that visible temple, from which Christ expelled the traffickers, and which he rebuilt with living stones, to the ever-lasting glory of God the Father.

We have the form: Bishops, priests, deacons: baptism, confirmation, eucharist: Bible, creed, catechism; commandments, excommunication, absolution: the Christian year, Christian week, Christian day. We have the form of the temple; the outline, the skeleton stands. And Christ comes to visit it. He finds the roof tiles slipped away, the windows broken, and in the walls great gaps everywhere, filled with cobwebs. Where are the living stones—the stones which Jesus himself put in their places to abide? How can God be honoured here in England, with such a universal treason on every hand?

What can we say to the complacent Anglican, who thinks it a matter of private convenience, whether he should even stand by his fellow Christians in Sunday worship? Who calls the creed of his Church in question, and that before unbelievers? Who has never bothered to ask the vicar of his parish, whether there is anything he ought to be doing to help? Who will think he does a very Christian thing, to let the Church marry him, and a very reasonable thing, to let the state divorce him? Some arguments dry up in the mouth, because they are too obvious to plead. What would you do, if you were told to argue for fifteen minutes, that black isn't white? And how am I to spend a sermon in arguing that treason is no true loyalty?

But it is no use, is it, my being one-sided? People who declare with passion that there is no argument on the other side confute themselves: for if there is nothing against them, it's a walk-over: and if it's a walk-over, what are they shouting about? And of course there *is* an argument on the other side in the present case: an argument which embodies a tragic mistake, but is no less powerful for that, to influence men's minds. There is the argument which opposes the form to the spirit: which says that, anyhow in religion, action must be the expression of previous inspiration. I must not profess the creed, because I may not have been inspired with a lively faith in all the articles.

I must not accept rules, for fear I should carry them out in the spirit of a slave or of a Pharisee. I must not make it my law to worship God, because it may turn out on any given day, that I have no more prayer in me than an old squeezed orange.

That is how some argue. It is not, of course, how they act. On any given occasion, they do not really say: I lack the inspiration to worship God today; they say, George is driving down to Bognor and he's offered me a place. But then they say: I should indeed lack the inspiration to worship God every week. If I worship him when there's nothing else to do, it will come out about right: in fact, God probably laid George on with his little M.G., to save me from trying to worship him too often.

Well, but if I go to Church, I'll be bored, and I shall scarcely pray. True enough, you'll be bored: and I dare say your spiritual resources are very limited. You'll be bored: but God will be publicly honoured or—put it negatively—at least he won't be publicly insulted: and you, for his honour, will have endured to be bored. And what will be the effect of your being bored? Don't you see that the effect of it is to throw you back on God? Why are you bored? Where are your spiritual resources? This is to make you know—I must be born again: or rather, since you have been born again, in the fount of your baptism—I must dig away the stony rubbish, and let out afresh the fountain of living waters, which God has opened there, that it might spring up to eternal life.

We are loyal to the form for the honour of God, because he is gracious, because his mercy endures for ever, because there is nothing better that a man can do, than glorify him. But the keeping of the form drives us back upon the Spirit: and the Spirit fills the form with life. Then God walks in his temple, and the house is peopled with cherubim: then heaven descends to earth, and earth is exalted to heaven: in the praises of him from whom all things everlastingly proceed, and to whom they unfailingly return, glory above glory, light beyond light, life uncreated, love immortal.

SOUL-MAKING

—preached on Whitsunday in Little St Mary's, Cambridge

Dons, or anyhow literary dons, are much too interested in words. Sensible people don't think about words except when they can't find the words they want. Otherwise they see straight through the words into the things the words convey. But from time to time we hear a phrase which astonishes us by its oddity and gives us pause. Maybe the speaker has no notion of saying anything beyond the ordinary. What is a cliché in English may be a paradox in French, and *vice versa*. If you remark to an old-fashioned Frenchman that he has, in his later years, got more serious than he used to be, he may reply, '*Il faut enfin faire son âme, n'est-ce pas?*'—As one's day declines, one can no longer put off making a job of one's soul. I should think *make one's soul* to be a mistranslation. No Christian, not even the most ironical Frenchman, can talk about *making his soul*; it goes too near to blasphemy. I take it '*faire son ame*' is more like '*faire les cheveux*': 'doing your soul' is like 'doing your hair', or, if you are a woman or a certain sort of American, 'doing your face'. You didn't make your features, God made them, but it is up to you to present them in good order. And so with your soul. You must get to work on it.

A limited, down-to-earth point of view, perhaps; but one that has the merit of being practical. There is to be no nonsense about this sort of religion, no waiting for the tide of feeling to flow or the light of inspiration to break. Your soul's a job; get on with it. When I was confirmed there came into my hands a little book of Tractarian provenance containing lists of things one should know for one's soul's health—the three parts of penitence, the four last things, the seven deadly sins, and so on. Among the rest there was the day's spiritual *menu*, which ran as follows:

> Remember, Christian Soul, that thou hast this day
> A God to glorify, a Christ to imitate,
> A soul to save, a body to mortify,

Sins to repent, virtues to acquire,
Hell to avoid, heaven to merit,
Eternity to prepare for, time to profit by,
Neighbours to edify, a world to despise,
Devils to combat, passions to subdue,
Death maybe to suffer, and judgement to undergo.

Well, even if I am let off death today and judgement tomorrow, it's certainly an assignment; and when I look through it I don't see which of the items I can hope to skip. So when I do my teeth and do my hair, let me not be negligent to do my soul.

But it's a puzzling task, surely. If a girl does her face, she does it to the satisfaction of the eyes which she glues to her looking-glass; if she can please herself, it is enough—herself, and the mob of friends or acquaintances of whom she is vaguely aware, as looking through her eyes. 'It'll do' means 'It'll do for them' or more narrowly, perhaps, 'for him'. But if I am to do my soul, it is no use making it up to meet my own eyes, still less, my neighbours'. I have to meet the unfathomable eyes of God. Merely to look that way, merely to uncover myself to those eyes, is half the business of doing my soul. And then, as to the other half—how am I to do it? What am I to do about it? Does my Maker want me to make up a face, or to put on an act? To profess before him virtuous intentions not grounded in my heart? I cannot make myself as God would wish to see me; I can only, under the look of his eyes, hope to see myself somewhat as he does see me. And how does he see me? With perfect truth, and with all the kindness in the world.

I must do my dressing (*faut faire sa toilette*): I must do my soul (*faut faire son âme*)—if such language is to be endured. And is it to be endured? Am not I unfaithful to my commission in talking so? I should be expounding scripture, not drawing out a Gallic parallel which is popish, profane, and utterly unbiblical. Do you think so? If you do, you put me on my mettle, and you drive me to a text. With the Apostle too it is getting-up time: 'The night is passing,' he says, 'the day is at hand: let us put off the works of darkness and put on the accoutrements of light. Let us go about in good order, as in the day.'—'Put on the Lord Jesus Christ,' he adds, 'and stop working out how to get the things you happen to feel like.' St Paul's text is very far from standing alone: it is a commonplace of the Epistles, that we have an outward person to array in clothes, and an inward person to clothe with virtues. St Paul does not say '*Fais ta toilette et fais ton âme*' because he doesn't happen to be writing French. But he does say, 'It is the daybreak of the world; put off the night and put on Jesus Christ.'

To put on Jesus Christ is not like dressing to please yourself; it is not like putting on the suit which the shopman persuaded you to think was *you*; it is more like putting on an academical gown, or the vestments of a priest; like accepting a character assigned you by your status, the character of a Christian. But that is not all; for Christ is not a set of lifeless habiliments, only brought alive, as our daily clothes are, by our living ourselves into them. Christ is his own living self; indeed, Christ is life itself. Even when he sees this most strongly, St Paul can hang on to his figure of speech. But it means that the clothes we put on must be seen as magic clothes. Instead of a live man putting on dead clothes, a dead man puts on living clothes which grow into him, transform him, and bring him to life. 'We that are in this tent of flesh,' he says, 'groan under our oppression—not that we wish to throw off our mortal raiment, but to be clothed over, that the mortal may be swallowed up in life.' That is what it is like, to put on the Lord Jesus Christ.

Language here has been stretched until it is tortured; and while the result moves our awe and our amazement, it does not perhaps help us very clearly to answer the question. What do I do to be saved? For how do I put on the Lord Jesus Christ? Try turning back a page from the text I quoted last. You have St Paul already at his spiritual toilette, but this time he is looking into a looking-glass. Here too there is magic. 'We all with unveiled face gazing into the reflection of the Lord's glory are transformed into the same image from one glory to another.' The glass shows us no face of ours; it shows us the face of our glorious Lord. And the relation of looking-glass to gazer is reversed: instead of the mirror-image taking form from the gazer's face, the gazer's face takes form from the image, changed from glory to glory under the radiance of the Lord's Spirit.

After all, then, we do not have to 'put on the Lord Jesus Christ', for he puts himself upon us. When we have found the eyes of God in the magic glass, there is nothing we have to do, so as to 'do our soul' in front of such a mirror; the mirror itself will do our soul.

And now suppose we try to answer the practical question, 'How is a Christian responsible for his own sanctification—for the making

of his soul?' What are we to say? From one point of view he is as
responsible for it as he is for keeping his bodily man in good order.
Unless I do my soul as regularly as I do my hair or my teeth, nothing
much is going to happen towards my sanctification. But I am not
responsible for my sanctification in the sense that I can sanctify myself by direct action. A woman can do her face, a Christian cannot
do his soul like that. He can look into the magic glass and be transformed by the Spirit of the Lord. But once again—if that is all,
nothing much will happen, either; mere gazing will not do it. The
vision in the glass, as St James reminds us, issues in practical inspirations or commands; and these we must go forth and obey; we
are responsible for our obedience. If prayer issues in no resolutions,
and if no resolutions are ever kept, little will happen towards our
sanctification.

And now, before I end, I ought perhaps to say something more
about that gazing into the glass of God; for so to talk may sound
high faluting and mystical and not for us. Let me explain. We use
such high-flown language to do justice, if we can, to the divine
reality. This, we must confess, is what is really going on. It is not
what we commonly see to be going on, blind as we are. But faith
cannot bear to measure God's glory or his grace by our blindness
in perceiving it.

We see no magic glass, and attempts to conjure up visual pictures
of our Saviour's face are of limited value. The plainest thing I can
say is that to look at our Lord just means to talk to him in all serious-
ness about himself. You might think of him at this season as he
actually is—the Ascended Christ who sends the Holy Ghost. You
might talk to him about that perfect union with his Father which he
now enjoys—union of mind, as well as of heart, of knowledge as
well as of will; and the overflowing happiness of simple oneness with
the living Truth he had always devotedly served. By talking to him
about himself you let him come into your mind—I do not say, into
your soul, for he was there already. But as you employ your thought
about him in speaking to him, he will become your thought, and you
will adore him. Presently you will see what he would have you do,
or not do. Make your resolution, and next time you pray, see if you
have kept it.

Even now what I have said sounds too ecstatic. Prayer can seem
dull or difficult; though if we give ourselves to it, it commonly ends
up less dull and less obstructed than it began. Only what is dull or

dark or laboured on our side is not so on the side of God, who rejoices in every least motion of our good will towards him; and where we see the merest vestige of his presence, there with cherubim and seraphim and all the host of heaven is he.

ALWAYS BEGINNING

—preached in Keble College Chapel, 1968

Shakespeare's foresters, you will remember, found 'books in the running brooks, sermons in stones, and good in everything'. There is an (I suspect legendary) German commentator who remarked how obvious here was the corruption of the text; the words had got transposed. The poet could not have written such nonsense. It must have originally been 'stones in the running brooks; sermons in books' and so forth. There has, I am afraid, been a good deal of emendation of this variety inflicted not only on Shakespeare but on the Bible. Here is the writer of Ecclesiastes saying 'God has made everything fair in its season' (has, that is, in Shakespeare's phrase, put good in everything): 'moreover he has put the world in men's mind, so that man cannot find out the work God has done from beginning to end.' Nonsense, the commentators have said. If God puts the world in men's mind, that cannot be the reason for their *not* tracing out his handiwork. If that were God's good pleasure, he would have taken the world out of men's mind, not put it in. It's all right, though; we have only to give a flick to the tail of a Hebrew letter, and hey presto, the word 'world' becomes the word 'ignorance'. That must be what the author wrote. Though God has made everything fair in its season, he has put nescience in men's mind, so that man cannot find out the work of God from start to finish. Splendid, a resounding platitude. Ignorance leads to ignorance. The sermons are tied back into the books, the stones into the running brooks, and we can all go to bed happy.

But I wonder. Wasn't Shakespeare, and wasn't Ecclesiastes, being a bit more subtle? If God had dumped a simple piece of knitting into our laps, we might hope to see how it goes from start to finish, and go on with the job ourselves. But he has thrown the world into our laps—and what an assignment! No wonder if we can't unravel it, nor make out the handiwork of God from start to finish, or see what hand we are to take in it. God might not have put the world in our mind. He might have made our minds a perfect blank to everything but a few simple little matters directly affecting us; as is the case, we may suppose, with the beasts of the field. But no, he had to put the world in our mind, and hence comes our bafflement.

It's a stock theme, of course, with the Hebrew prophets and especially the book of Isaiah. The man of God cracks off at us a whole series of rhetorical questions: what do we know? Can we track the wind? Can we weigh the earth in a balance? I get somewhat hot under the collar when these passages are read out in chapel because the reply to so many queries expecting the answer 'no' is now 'yes'. I, Austin Farrer, cannot track the winds, but it's no great mystery to the meteorologists. I cannot weigh the earth in a balance, but an astronomer (or would it be a geophysicist?) is ready to state its substantial mass, which is, I suppose, what the prophet means. I listen to the reading out of the prophet's eloquence, and wonder how many of the bodies in chapel will go away with the impression that the scientists have taken over the job of being God.

It is certainly a propaganda nuisance that the unanswerable posers of the Hebrew prophets are physical commonplaces now: but that's all it is. No reflective person can doubt that the puzzles we are aware of are far more numerous and more baffling than theirs were. The more we know, the more we see we don't. And that may be taken to be the point of Ecclesiastes' remark: God has put the world in men's minds, so that man is baffled to find out the work God has done first and last: and the more world he has thrown at us, the more baffled we are. If a modern Isaiah wants to point the lesson of our ignorance, he has only to mention the confines of the universe, or the ultimate constituents of matter: as Pascal said, the infinitely great, the infinitely small. If we go to the moon, we have gone, perhaps, further than the roof of Ecclesiastes' imagined world: but in relation to the ceiling of things, as we now see it, we've done no more than lift our hand to scratch our own heads.

God has put the world in our mind, and so it is that we are always on the threshold of knowledge. The decisive advance is the next step forward, or the step after that; then we shall really have things under control. Even more, God has put God into our mind, and therefore we are always beginning, always on the verge of possession. For here the case is, in a way, even more extreme. Science can cut off bits or aspects from the world and master them: the steps that really matter may always be the steps yet to be taken, but the steps of our previous progress are at least real and our results assured. But God is all of a piece: you cannot take pieces from God and master him bit by bit. And so in our pilgrimage to God we never seem to have made even an assured beginning. All's to do afresh and we have to stretch ourselves for the embrace of the infinite every day anew. The most advanced of saints commonly think that they have got nowhere. Looking back, they see with thankful amazement what God has done in or through them; they see themselves as far as ever from laying hold on God.

Christians must wish to be able to edify their less believing friends by claiming some fruits of religion, some experience of God. But take care; it's a dangerous proceeding and may end in professions very destructive to the person who makes them. It would be better to say, Don't take me for anything more than what you find me: I'm not much of a man, am I? I'll tell you about a real Christian I once knew . . . Some undergraduates have made me talk three times this term about how one can pray. Well, thank goodness that's over. It's a fine thing, indeed, for two Christians to talk together about praying. But if one is put up to pontificate about it how can one avoid being put in the absurd position of talking like a man who can pray? And no one can pray, or at least not I, for to pray is to embrace that infinite Godhead which God has put in our mind. We are always on the threshold of prayer: and indeed it is a marvellous thing to have been admitted so far, to have a crack of the door open, and half a foot on the sill: but it is always in the future, that we shall make something of the beginning which has been so mercifuly allowed to us.

Even the dear Christ who saves us was never in this mortal life further forward than a beginning. I do not say that he made no more than a beginning of knowing God our Father. Indeed no, I do not say that. But Jesus had set his heart on the kingdom of God — that God's infinite goodness should infinitely and in all things prevail — God's will be done on earth, just as it is expressed in his heavenly mind. And Jesus could make but a beginning of it, there and then — the dawn was breaking, the sun would presently arise; things took a mighty move towards the great consummation, when he died on the cross, and rose from the dead. There was opened up a new and living way to God — but still it remained for God's creatures to find it and march up it.

There are people now who profess the Christian name, and who

are nevertheless ashamed of heavenly hope. The cry is raised, 'A
this worldly religion.' There *may* be a bonus hereafter—only better
not count on it. But I tell you that Christianity cannot for any length
of time survive the amputation of such a limb as life to come. For
God has put his infinity in our mind, and if we cannot stretch out
for him beyond the little beginnings here allowed us, we must let
go of God and loose him wholly. For we can only have God, if God
has us: and if he will not make a job of us and bring us to union with
his glorious infinity, how can we believe that he has taken hold of us
at all? What is our salvation, but that we are in the hands of God?
And what are the hands of God, if they are weaker than animal
death?

This life is always a beginning, no more—and therefore it's
heaven or nothing for us. But again—for the same reason, because
of the infinity of God—heaven itself is always a beginning: a beginning, indeed, which for those that are there has really and firmly
begun: the exploration of a Paradise of which more will always be
before us than what we have seen. So that the loveliness we have
known always increases our desire for the delight to which it points
and leads us on; as we walk the way we are drawn into the very
thought and action of God. We sing all too Jewishly of heaven, as a
perpetual Sabbath: but the Sabbath was the seventh day; the
closure of the week. Shall not we call heaven Sunday, an endless
beginning, ceaseless wonder, perpetual resurrection in the unex-
hausted power of him who everlastingly makes all things new? Be
sure of this, there is no coming to the end of God; the more we
know of him and his ways, the more avenues will open for further
exploration, or revelation, rather: we may explore God's creatures,
but God is known as he bestows himself.

To return to earth—it's the end of the Church's year, and we may
well do some self-examination and see how we have spent our time
and how we have served our Creator. We shall find that all is to be
begun again—who can say we have advanced? But we must be
patient. God shapes us by his providence and by our very failures,
if we will keep looking to him. He knows that the beginnings he
has made with us are not in vain. For it is his good pleasure to give
us the kingdom.

FATHERS' SONS

—preached in Keble College Chapel, 1968

There is a celebrated and ancient mythological poem which a Fellow of this College is at present editing in a manner which is going to bring him much credit and us, we hope, a glimmer of reflected glory. This ancient poet, the object of his studious care, seizes every opportunity for rhetorical description: but there is no episode that gives him greater scope than the scene of the world going on fire. Everything burns: the mountain forests blaze like torches, the lakes and seas dry and the fishes die gasping: all the sonorous names on the ancient world map spring out of the poet's page in letters of flame as the irresistible terror sweeps from east to west. Splendid stuff—but what's it all about? Why the universal holocaust? It is all along of that foolish Phaethon. He was, his mother told him, the offspring of the Sun-god; but it's a wise child that knows its own father and when he was taunted with the fishiness of such a tale he sought out his divine parent and asked for a sure token of his paternity. The god said he'd show them. 'Ask me anything you like, my boy, and I'll do it for you,' he said, adding an oath it was impossible for a god to revoke. And the wretched boy asked to do his father's work for a day—to drive the chariot of the Sun up the road of sky. And so—but why go on? You can do the rest of the story for yourselves, even supposing you don't know it already.

The myth of Phaethon bears on its face a startling resemblance to a recurrent theme of St John's Gospel. Here too is one who claims the God of Light for his Father. His claim is contested; and how does he uphold it? 'If I do not do the works of my Father, believe me not.' Or again; 'the Father loves the Son and shows him whatsoever work he does!' 'If you do not believe me, believe me for the very works' sake.' And the dénouements of the story are similar. For doing his father's work, Phaethon falls in flaming ruin from the sky; for doing *his* Father's work, Jesus is crucified.

There's a similarity in theme, yes; but there's an enormous dif-

ference in spirit. Phaethon proves himself the son of Light by pre-
vailing on Helius to break the serene continuity of his blessed work,
and violate the covenant of day and night. Jesus shows whose Son
he is by utter identification with the Father's work, which has been
from the beginning and which proceeds unbroken to its consummation. Especially revealing, perhaps, is the exchange between Jesus
and the Jews over the healing on Sabbath. To heal, they hold, is to
work; and man must not work on Sabbath. He must imitate his
Creator, who made the world in six days' work, and on the seventh
rested. But Jesus calmly says: 'My Father is at work until now, and
so am I.' The story of creation then, is a story, whatever it may
mean, concerned with the origin and first institution of things. But
the blessed parent and sole begetter of all creatures is ceaselessly at
work in the world he has made: at work in nature, at work in salvation. The Son of God is known by this, that this work is shown to
him and it carries him along with it, to do it.

We are talking of beginnings. Where does Christ begin from, in
that dedicated action in which he calls us all to participate? He
begins from the beginning: not from the day of his finding that his
Father's house was his house when he was twelve years old; not
from the day of his baptism and heavenly call, not from the forty
days of his wilderness retreat: no, he identified himself with what
was before his birth, indeed, before Abraham's; with the beginning
of God's mighty purpose for all things: from where *God* had begun
with him.

Not so Phaethon. He is nervously anxious for a brand-new beginning to be made for *him*: then he will know and everyone will
know, that he is the child of God.

Well, will you be a Christian or a Phaethonian? The modern
Phaethonian says: how do I know the whole thing isn't a sham?
How do I know I have a Father in heaven? I must somehow find
him, and pray to him (and so far the Phaethonian isn't all that off
the mark). And I must get him to do something very plain and
evident for me. He must make me feel quite different (and so he will,
but not like this). He must cure my weaknesses, and make me
strong (and so he will, but not like this).

Such is the Phaethonian's approach: and what is the Christian's?
He also prays, no doubt, and . . . I wish I knew how I was to say
this. Let me grasp at something real, which some of you at least
know something of, and so do I. Late in the last vacation sixteen

members of the College went into retreat. They went into retreat, and, as happens in retreat, they went into silence, to give themselves a chance of attending for once to what this foolish busy life of ours perpetually interrupts. They came out of their silence in due course, and considered what they had discovered; and one after another gave the apparently empty answer, that they had discovered silence itself.

The answer was only empty in appearance: for when they explained themselves it became clear that what they meant was this; that man's silence is God's presence. If the clouds are swept away, no one needs to paint blue into the sky or furnish the depth of space with the majestic procession of sun, moon and stars. The curtain of cloud being once withdrawn, these things are there; and when the din of trivial thought is still, and this turmoil of petty lusts and cares I call myself is pushed aside, then God is there.

Of course: and you are perfectly right. It is, in a sense, a simple discovery; yet the odd thing is, it comes new to us, over and over again. It's a discovery you can read of in the lives of saints over many centuries: and doubtless what dawns on you dawned on Christ like the daybreak of the world, when he knelt in the Galilean hills, and opened his heart.

God is there. But in what manner is he there? God is the mystery of mysteries: he is invisible to sense, inapprehensible even to thought. But he is present in his work, his infinite action: unresting, unhasting, and silent as light: making, sustaining, guiding, perfecting, redeeming. Phaethon looked up, and saw the wheel of the visible sky changelessly turning, and he longed to put his spoke into it. Christ looked through, and saw the loving work of a Father, bringing to glory the creatures of his hand; he saw what was his own place in that work, and gave himself to it.

What is it, then? God's beginning with us is from everlasting; our beginnings are no more than our ceasing to ignore what God has begun before us, in us, through us. Well, but the clouds of ignorance close in again; the fuss and business of life returns.

How do I *keep* before my eyes the work of God? As a Christian, I know two things about that work. What God does is what is done by Christ and in Christ, in those acts of his which the Apostles' Creed summarises. But I know also that what God does is being done here and now; his holy will challenges me in every present need, and calls me in every attraction of goodness. God's work is my neighbour, God's work is my soul. The secret of being a Christian lies in holding these two extremes together: Christ in the Gospel; our present existence here. We must hold them together, for God's work, so far as it concerns us men, is one work: one, though manifold. It is the fulfilment of Christ, in head and members: Christ in the gospel and in the height of heaven; Christ in us, the hope of glory.

I must open my heart to both, and know them for one, and then I shall be open to the work of God. How shall I do it? By two most necessary exercises of Christian prayer. One is plain enough. It is intercession. There is no need to tell you what that is. You know you must pray for your fellowmen. But perhaps it will add something to so plain a duty, if we see it as an identification of ourselves with what God is working, and has been at work upon from the beginning. To know what God is doing in our neighbour—yes, and in our own soul—and to go heartily along with it by God's inspiration—that would be to pray indeed, would it not?

But I am putting the cart before the horse. The other exercise of prayer comes first, for Christ comes first in the work of God and it is by seeing what is done in him that we have the clue to see what is done in our world of men. I suppose we have now reached the point in the sermon when you are all asleep, and yet what I am going now to say is the only piece, I should think, that it would do you any good to remember. We can find the heart and substance of the work of God, which is Christ, by praying the scenes of the Gospel. Set Jesus before you in any one of the great scenes of his life. He stands in the waters of Jordan and accepts his calling to so strange a work. He conquers temptation in the wilderness. He calls disciples to share his calling. How shall I complete such a catalogue? Above all, there are the scenes of his passion, and his glorious resurrection. Take any such scene, with the written word to help you — and—this is the great point—do not begin preaching yourself a sermon on your duty as resulting from what you read but do your best to go into the mind and heart of Jesus as he is there presented, and there occupied. See what his attitude is, what is the set of his will and the movement of his love towards his Father or his fellow men: and identify yourself, let yourself go with it. That requires no self-consciousness, no separate and special doing. We identify ourselves with what we adore; the heart that can love Christ is in Christ's keeping.

Perhaps God's eternal predestinating thought is too distant a beginning for us, and it is enough we should go back into that beginning he made with us in Christ before the grandfathers of our eldest oaks took root in our land; and when we turn back to pray for ourselves and, even better, for our friends, we shall find no strangeness, no breach, no discontinuity, between the Christ portrayed in the Gospel, and the Christ fashioned in mankind.

And if we Christians could but pray so, then a better fire than Phaethon's would surely run across the world. Know Christ, and you will know that there is no obstacle to his omnipotent love but men's ignoring it.

THE COMMANDER'S LOVE

We know an old naval officer, a huge and splendid man: to hear him blast an incompetent navigator out of his water would be an experience for the student of invective. I have heard him say—he likes to say it—he is a man who feels that if a point is worth making, it is worth repeating. So a parson is not likely to talk to him for long, without hearing something like this. 'Our chaplain isn't a bad fellow, but he will preach about the love of God. This sort of thing does a lot of harm. Makes religion sound so unnatural. A man can't love God, I mean to say. Perfect nonsense. I love my wife, I honour God and I hope I obey him: as I do the Admiral, and the Queen. If only the parsons would stick to commonsense, the men would pay a lot more attention to what they say.' So says the commander, and one can't help feeling sorry for his chaplain: the commander is so large and authoritative, and has such a bridge to his nose, that nose under which the chaplain has to preach, has to preach, poor man, the Gospel he has been ordained to deliver; has to tell the men, whether they like it or not, that fornication kills the soul; and to tell the commander, whether he likes it or not, that (since he says he means to obey God, if he can) the first precept laid on him is this: Thou shalt love the Lord thy God with all thy heart, and all thy soul, with all thy mind and all thy strength.

Poor chaplain, he's got to preach the word of God, whatever the commander says: but how is he to persuade the commander? How is a man to love the Great Cause of all, the mind behind the universe? He'd find it hard work to love his wife, if she hadn't got a mouth, and a pair of eyes. Make her invisible, reduce her to a speaking voice, and she'd be a queer object to love, even though she had a human mind like her husband, and sympathies attuned to his. Love goes by kindness, that is, by kinship. How shall we love a God who is not only invisible, but inaudible, and at the same time infinitely wise, and great? You would scarcely have the nerve to tell that hard-bitten old commander that he can draw a picture in his mind, and fall in love with that: the picture, let us say, of a fatherly man with a majestic forehead sitting on a throne. That is just the sort of thing that the commander reckons to be nonsense, only fit for parsons and schoolgirls. And if you say, but what about Jesus Christ, he replies, that he respects him very much; that he taught us how to live, and backed his teaching by his example: but that to us he's a man in a book, and you can't love a man in a book. At least, ordinary people can't: it may be different for these literary fellows. And as for imagining him in the room with you, when you've read what he said, surely tricks like that can't be a necessary part of a sensible man's religion. So says the commander. And now I find my sympathies veering round from the chaplain to his officer; for there is something very straight and candid in what he says, and I feel that we ought to be able to meet him on his own ground. But how can we, since it is written: Thou shalt love the Lord thy God, and not only so: but, 'with all thy heart.'

It does not seem likely that the chaplain will persuade the commander. After all, commanders are unpersuadable, almost by definition. But perhaps, as Isaiah said to his unpersuadable young king, the Lord God himself will give him a sign. The commander, as he quite truthfully boasts, loves his wife, and he might have added, his four children no less. Now it happens that one of these dear beings falls ill, and is in some kind of danger. Then, not by any miracle, but by the ordinary processes of nature and medicine, the patient comes back, as though from the other side of a thick mist. The commander goes to divine service, and they begin saying one of those psalms about the great things God has done for us, and how he brings us back from the gates of death; and that high bridged and venerable nose is filled with tears. It seems one cannot sufficiently love a God who does such things for men; how foolish, how stubborn one has been, to keep him at a distance all these years.

But that is only the moment of sentiment: the hour of reflection follows. If we cannot help feeling the hand of God in the recovery of a dear endangered life, but overflow with thankfulness; why not be equally ready to feel the direct stab of divine cruelty in the boy's falling ill? And suppose—for boys do die—the boy had died? And anyhow we all do die in the end: so what's the odds?

The commander may leave it at that. I must say I should like to think that the chaplain would be at his elbow in that moment of reflection, that he had the commander's confidence, and knew what to say. But how seldom, alas, anything of that kind happens. The commander will probably have to sort it out himself, with the aid of an occasional verse from the psalms. No, says the commander to himself, it's an odd thing: they look the same, but they aren't the same. The bad things and the good things look as though they ought equally to be credited to God: but they don't make that impression. Acts of life-saving belong to him, they come straight from his heart; disaster and destruction are not his in the same way. We find ourselves asking not, why does he do them, but why does he let them happen? Bad things don't reveal a cruel God; they hide from us the God of love. I wish I could make sense of this—the world's such a mixture of bright and dark. If I could see the whole thing from start to finish as a process by which God is saving us, as, in the last three weeks, he has saved my young John, why then — why, then—how I wish the ship's chaplain were there, he would never have a better chance than this to preach the Gospel of saving love. For Christ's life, and death, and resurrection, show us this, that through all our existence, and all the circumstances of it, God is drawing us up from destruction to everlasting life. And progress in the Christian way should mean this, that we learn more and more to experience our life as the saving work of God.

The commander could not love God, we remember, because God was great and distant: it was otherwise when the hand of the Almighty touched him. But to the eyes of an enlightened faith, we are never out of the hands of God; every friend is a blessing, every duty a guidance, every necessity a call, every task a divine service. Taking these things right, we are saved from corruption and death, we are lifted to everlasting life, and into union with God himself.

I don't know whether you ever try to read the Book of Job. If so, what do you make of it? It is the description of a mental agony; as for the solution, and the happy ending, one can't help feeling that it has been clamped on by violence, like a happy ending added to *Hamlet* by an old-fashioned film producer. But what of Job's mental agony? For modern taste, it seems too much concerned with a worry about wicked men escaping their punishment, and righteous men failing of their reward: and most of us don't care whether the wicked are punished or not (except of course when the wicked attack us) nor yet whether the just are or are not rewarded (except, of course, when we see ourselves in the role of good men lacking due recognition). But really the whole question of kicks and halfpence is very superficial. It is, of course, meat and drink to Job's comforters, but Job has a deeper concern. Job has loved God, and wants to love him still: even more, he wants to have God loving him. But how can this be? God's love was shown in flocks and herds, in sons and daughters, and no less in the good and useful life he gave Job to live, as a magistrate and a patron of the poor. But one day has carried off the herds, killed the children and brought Job down from the seat of judgement to the dunghill. We can love no other God but a God revealed in his acts; and the love of God to us is itself action, no mere sentiment. Job is as a man whose friend has stabbed him—*Et tu, Brute?*—even now he would love God, if he could see any sense in it, if someone could show him why God should have done it.

It is no accident that the solution of the plot is no solution of the problem: without the revelation of Christ, there is no escape from Job's dilemma. If we are to love God, we must feel him in the whole substance of our life: we cannot love disembodied ghosts, and the whole world pressing in on us is the body, or better, let us say, the hand, through which God upholds, directs, checks and caresses us. And without Christ's revelation of redemptive suffering, and everlasting life, we should lack the voice which interprets to us the action of God's mysterious hands.

I have asked you what you make of Job—and now I am going to ask you about a New Testament puzzle. Have you noticed how many of the texts about love of God or love of Christ are ambiguous? To take one at random—St Paul prays for his Ephesians, 'that they may know the love of Christ, which passes knowledge'. What are they to know? What is this mysterious depth, which can be dipped into, but never plumbed? Is it the love of Christ for us? Or is it the blessedness of loving Christ? Or is it the Christ-love, that is, the love with which Christ inspires us, so that we love all things and all men somewhat as he loves them? Perhaps in this or that text careful reflection will enable you to decide—here it is Christ's love for us—there it is ours for him—and here again it is a Christ-love towards all. But other texts are hopelessly ambiguous. Ambiguous, yes: but why 'hopelessly'? What does it matter, after all? If the sacred writers were content with the ambiguity, it is because they feel no need to distinguish. These three loves are bound together: but the love of God for us comes first. Herein is love, not that we love God, but that he has loved us, and given his Son to be the propitiation for our sins. Once this love is present, and seen, and accepted, our love for God can scarcely fail, for it is his gift; and what form shall our love of God take—we soon come to an end of oh! and ah!—if it does not take the form of sympathising with his love towards his whole creation, and especially towards those of our fellows to whom he has bound us? There is no great need to distinguish between these three loves: to St Paul or St John divine love is the element in which the Christian lives, and of which the currents flow downward, upward, and outward on every hand.

THE BRETHREN FORGIVEN

When we had filled our copybooks at the infant-school I attended, they were given us to take home for our parents to admire. But my book had a page somewhere near the middle on which my teacher had scrawled a contemptuous comment. Pride forbade me to expose it to parental eyes; I was resolved to get rid of it. It was very awkward. You could not tear out one page without the other half of the sheet coming loose; and if I took that out too, an exercise would be seen to leave off in the middle of a word. Still, I risked it; I buried the incriminating sheet in a wet and leafy ditch on the walk back from school. I met my parents with burning cheeks. Nothing was said. But then I could not sleep. In my waking nightmare tiresome busybodies from the neighbourhood came round to the door and rang the bell. They carried the stained and soaking sheet still faintly decipherable in their outraged hands. After a week of this I could stand no more. I made my mother sit by my bed. I gave her three sobs to each syllable, but in the end I told her all. I was wondering when the lightning would fall; she I suppose, was wondering, dear woman, what she had done to make her child so frightened of her.

Joseph's brethren had much more rational grounds for fear. They had buried a clue which, so far from rotting away in a damp ditch, had been hauled up out of the dry cistern into which they had thrown it. It had trudged away on living feet, and carried a speaking tongue in its head. Being grown men, not tender little children, Joseph's brethren had got their consciences under control, and managed the burden of their secret guilt. But then would Joseph break from his servitude beyond the Sinaitic sands, and walk in to accuse them? True, their father was very old; perhaps he would convenience them by dying first; then they could deal with Joseph.

You must not think that the crime of the ten brethren was a crime they could not justify to themselves by any sort of rotten story. It was not just that they disliked the lad. He was the late-born son of a rival mother, Rachel, their father's darling. Their father showed every sign of setting him before his seniors, and giving him the best of the inheritance; and the wretched boy backed his chances by claiming to receive prophetic dreams, of which he was, of course, the hero; he saw himself as the head of the family, with the others cringing before his feet. It was an outrage on all natural justice: what about the rights and claims of Reuben's little children, or of Judah's? Were they to have the bread snatched from between their teeth, while Joseph swept the stakes? Was it not rather decent of them to sell him over the sand, and not just cut his throat? The story was as good as most of the stories we tell ourselves to justify our selfishness, or our disregard of others' claims. We can be wonderfully persuasive when we have ourselves for our sole audience; the orator is eloquent in his defence, and 'Hear hear!' resounds from all the benches of our inner parliament. That is just where grown men have it over children: they are far better at telling themselves moral lies. Unfortunately it was not themselves they had to convince, it was Joseph: and when it came to that, the whole story somehow looked very different.

As for Joseph, I'm afraid it must be confessed that his conduct was no better than human. His first idea was to compensate his pride by grinding his brethren in the dust. His second was to get Benjamin, his only full brother, Rachel's other child, away from them, and have him for his own. It was only when the attempt to carry that point drew from them an undisguised expression of anxiety for the effect on their father of losing so dear a child, that Joseph broke down and, in throwing off his disguise, forgave them. His forgiveness, when it came, was not without nobility. 'And now be not grieved or angry with yourselves that ye sold me hither: for God did send me before you, to preserve you a remnant on the earth, and to save you alive.' I am only sorry that, in sending them away to fetch their father, he could not resist the parting jab. 'See that ye come not to blows on the road.'

The Church reads the tale of Joseph and his brethren in parallel with the history of Christ's passion; and reflecting on the comparison, we may dare to wonder what sort of story the disciples of Jesus might have told themselves if they had not faced him, risen from the dead? They had deserted him. Well, it had been a noble enterprise, but it was doomed to failure. What good could it have done, after all—a futile act of solidarity, forcing the Governor to multiply crucifixions? What of their wives and children, left without support and under censure? Jesus had suffered alone. It was horrible, certainly, to think of those moments; but they had been comparatively brief. How could you weigh them against the rest of life? Judas, certainly, had gone too far. To put himself on the safe side of the law he had, like the patriarch Judah his namesake, sold a new Joseph to the Gentiles. But then his conscience had overcome him: he had hanged himself. They had done nothing so black; they were no worse than other men; surely, like others, they could live with their guilt—if guilt it was.

So they might—indeed, I think we may say, they must—have gone on all their lives, wondering whether they could quite forgive themselves. Only one person could finally forgive them, and that was the man they had betrayed. The matter, in fact, was quickly settled, when he who was reckoned the son of Joseph came back to them alive beyond all hope out of the waterless pit into which his body had been thrown. And then how aptly and more than aptly does the generosity of Joseph fit the lips of Christ! Be not grieved, or angry with yourselves, for what you did. It was the Father sending me before you, to preserve life . . . And how? Joseph had found means to feed the starving nations with inexhaustible bread. 'Work not for the food that perishes but for the food that nourishes to everlasting life,' said the new Joseph to his people: and this bread was to be his flesh, which he would give for the life of the world. Joseph's brethren had been only the remoter causes of his coming to save the food supply of the Levant; Jesus' disciples had played a more intimate part in the history which made the body of Christ a lifegiving sacrifice.

The people who are repelled by what they imagine Christianity to be, accuse us of spreading the melancholy doctrine that one cannot live without sinning. What's the use of bothering? they say. One can't move about without trampling the daisies; one must let oneself off, and go on doing one's best. Well, but the daisies we trample are other people's faces. Nor is it Christianity that makes it so; it's the fact, whatever Christians do or don't say. The news the Gospel brings us isn't this, for this isn't news at all. It's the oldest and stalest of commonplaces. The news is that the faces we trample can forgive us, as fast as we trample them. Christ embodies every man in himself, and makes all injuries his own: not only the injuries we do our neighbours by act or by neglect, but also the injuries we do to ourself, to the man in us whom God's creative hand designs to frame.

It is a poor thing indeed to let ourselves off; but to be forgiven readily and kindly by him who, having suffered all, has every right to forgive all; to receive the pardon of our victim, and our Maker: that is the Gospel of joy. 'Be not grieved or angry with yourselves for that ye sold me—through these things God sent me on before you, to preserve life.' And what a life-giving thing is Christ's forgiveness! In Lent we may be more careful to examine our lives; but, if we know how to find our Pardoner, it will not make us sad for long.

I do not want to seem to be selling you a line of party goods. But perhaps you have the curiosity to know what people who confess before a Christian priest find in it. I reply simply that we find Christ in it. Christ makes himself most effectively present for different purposes in different ways. To feed us with his body, he gives us bread and wine. To inform us with his mind, he gives us the Scriptures. To confront our sins, and to speak our pardon, he uses a man of flesh and blood. You know that our Church offers you the opportunity, and does not constrain you to use it, unless you are so defeated in your life as to forsake the altar. Then it is a duty to seek the priest. Otherwise it is open to your free choice. And I wish I could convey to those who do not know by experience, how much happiness, and what life-giving power, resides in this sacrament.

But whether you find Christ in his priest, or somehow in your heart, do not neglect confession or go without the assurance of forgiveness; it is the everlasting spring of renewal, the miracle that does not fail.

LEAD US NOT INTO TEMPTATION

In speaking on such a text as this there is no need to make pretty introductions or fish about for the interest of a languid audience. If you hoped nothing from God, even with half your heart, you would not be here: and if you hope anything from God, you hope what Jesus in these words encourages you to pray for. Perhaps you do not know God personally enough to care greatly whether he forgives you or not, so 'forgive our trespasses' will go over your head. Perhaps you are too knowing, too sophisticated and too secure to rely on God for the provision of daily need; you can afford to leave 'Give us this day our daily bread' to Africans and Asiatics. But unless your self-confidence is positively fatuous you know that you stand in danger of self-betrayal, of being frustrated by your own weakness or blindness.

'Lead us not into temptation.' Temptation is what distracts us, beguiles us or bullies us off the path. Temptation is what makes real life different from the world of our dreams. We dream a world which is wax under the moulding of our ambitions or of our aspirations; we meet a world which faces us with trials we have not the character to surmount, and with seductions we have not the virtue to resist. And so our achievement never has been what we hoped, nor has our self been the person that we desired. We shall be mere pipe-dreamers if we imagine that our personal future will be quite unlike our personal past: and so the cry 'Lead us not into temptation' must rise to our lips if we have any sense whatever of a God to whom we can pray.

Naturally, the particular light in which we view temptation will vary according to the aims we entertain. If we were heroic saints, our single desire would be to fulfil God's good pleasure, and our deep distress would be that we were constantly frustrated of our aim. As it is, our heartfelt aspirations are probably nothing so exalted, and there is no poison to the spiritual life like the poison of pretending desires we do not have. Still, we would passionately

like to be nobler creatures than we are, and still more passionately
to succeed in an effective concentration on our less trivial ambitions;
and so, if there is a God to help us, we shall cry to him from the
heart, 'Do we have to keep being sidetracked and defeated like this?
Lead us not into temptation, but rescue us from mischief.'

'Lead us not into temptation.' Ah, but would God in any case
lead us into temptation? How dare I ask God to be good or beg the
Father of mercy to refrain from satanic malice? St James is the
spokesman of our natural feeling when he roundly says, 'Let not
any man that is tempted say, "I am tempted of God"; for God is
untempted of evil, and himself tempts no man. Every man is tempted
when he is drawn away by his own passion and enticed.' So says
St James, and we think it commonsense; only wondering perhaps
how one who professes himself the servant of Jesus Christ could
find authority for contradicting the Lord's Prayer. Where could he
find his authority? He could find it in the Lord's Prayer itself, and
in the very next phrase. Lead us not into temptation *but rescue us
from the wicked fiend*. So after all it is the wicked fiend who tempts
(and, by the way, there is no doubt that the evil from which the
prayer asks deliverance is personally meant). What we ask of the
divine goodness is, therefore, that he should rescue us from our
enemy and his: not that he should refrain from putting our virtue
through destructive tests.

It is the second half of my text, not the first, which marks out the
starting-point of living religion. I was shown the other day a dis-
tressing passage in Dr Leslie Rouse's autobiography. It transcribes
an old letter, almost too painful to be read, from a relative of his, a
simple countrywoman, who has lost a young child. She complains
of the unendurable agony imposed on her by the ancestral belief
that whatever happens is the direct will of God Almighty. It is intolerable to see the perfect little body deprived of life; it is double
torment to have to think that God has done it to you. Be rid of the
monstrous hypothesis, deny God, and you can reach some kind of
peace.

One cannot disagree with the conclusion: only one can point out
that the unhappy mother has stood religion on its head. We do not
begin with the assurance that everything is under the hand of
almighty providence. We begin from a world touched with glories
and shot through with agonies, and we call upon the God of glory
to deliver us from the wicked fiend. The bereaved mother who has

no God to implore is in no better case, far from it, than one who believes in him. Their miseries are equal; but one calls on a saviour, the other grins and bears it. Religion begins with the God of Salvation; and we do not ask him to save us from himself, we ask him to save us from our enemy and his. Whether we personify the forces of evil or not is a side-issue. If we do personify them as Satan, we are at least clear that we do not identify them with God. As with disasters, so with temptations; they are not the direct inflictions of a divine pastoral strategy, twisting our tails for the good of our souls. God does not need to invent temptations for us; the waywardness of our desire, the low standards of our neighbours, the cross-accidents inevitable in a world of creatures freely moving, will provide us enough trials and to spare. We cry to the God of Salvation to rescue us from the mischief which would else frustrate our worthy purposes.

Very well; and perhaps that is more than half the truth. But it can't be the whole of it; or why did divine lips teach us to say, 'Lead us not into temptation?' There is a deep mystery here; but it is a mystery we cannot afford to neglect. What shall we say? We shall say that the very faith which calls on an invincible saviour must credit him with an ultimate control. Why is it that neither the cruel malice of demons nor the disastrous folly of men, neither the adversity of circumstance nor the collapse of life itself can defeat the saving power of God? It is because demons and men, nature and history are his creations, and by an invisible skill which is the very masterpiece of providence he bends them to his purposes. However puzzling it may be to reason, it is the vital freedom of faith to move on two planes, and to feel everywhere a double action: the action of created forces, often out of control, and defying God; and the action of God shaping them as a raw material, and making them the stuff of a higher good.

Put it abstractly like that and it sounds no better than a piece of verbal pomposity or of philosophical pretence. That is why it is so fortunate for us that the living truth is not presented to us in flat-footed generalisations.

Here, in St Matthew's Gospel, is Jesus teaching us to pray against temptation: and if we can pray and think like Jesus we who are Christians may be well content. He knew what he was saying, for he knew temptation; he alone, through purity of heart, was able to strip its false colours and see it for what it was. He teaches us to pray against temptation, and his teaching is in the Sermon on the

Mount, between his two recorded temptations—his visionary temptation in the wilderness, and the all too physical ordeal of his cross.

Let us ask, then, who or what tempted Jesus in the wilderness? Satan tempted him. Yes, no doubt; and yet it is also written, 'The Spirit of God drove him into the wilderness to be tempted by the devil.' And who can fail to see the hand of a divine purpose in those visionary contests, through which the faithful sonship of Jesus to his Father achieved so perfect an expression.

Then to apply the same question to the more crushing temptation —who faced Jesus with the ordeal of the cross? Caiaphas, Pilate, Iscariot. Yes, but said Jesus, the Son of Man must suffer, and by that path enters into his glory. The death of Christ was the redemption of the world; and if the hand of God was not in that event then where are we to look for it?

I said that it was not in the vapid generality of speculation, but in the living particularity of action, that the truth has been disclosed to us; and now we come to the fine point of the matter. If Satan in the wilderness, or if his minions at Jerusalem, served the purposes of eternal salvation, how did they do so? Why, by driving Jesus to prayer, and throwing him into the arms of his Father, his Saviour and his God. He prayed to be delivered, and he was delivered, though not as flesh and blood account deliverance; not from but through the death he shuddered at; and his deliverance delivered us all.

Jesus calls on us to pray, that we may not be brought into temptation, but rescued from the wicked fiend; and evidently it is no secondary matter that we should so pray. For it is by so praying, and by so trusting, that we allow God the victory over his enemy, and give occasion to that divine miracle, and masterpiece of wonders, which brings out of evils permitted a good designed, and out of death life immortal.

THE HIDDEN SPRING

The Holy Communion is not a special part of our religion, it just is our religion, sacramentally enacted. Of course God is not served only by the celebration of sacraments, but much more by an obedience to his practical commands. But in so far as our religion receives sacramental enactment, it is all summed up in the Eucharist, no aspect of it is left out. For the whole of our religion is summed up in Christ, and the sacrament presents Christ, his birth, death, resurrection, and his present existence: his manhood and his godhead, his being in himself, and the service of his Father.

Since the Eucharist is so many-sided, almost anything may be a fit theme for a meditation in preparation of it. Through Christ we are to approach God, and so we shall make a better communion if we come with an enlivened idea of the God we are to approach. Let us take this most fundamental point. Let us reflect together on the being of God.

I want to find God, to lay my hands, as it were, on the reality of God, to know him not in idea, but in substance. Where is he, then? I am taught to say, everywhere. But how 'Everywhere'? Not like the atmosphere; not like a diffused ghostly being flowing through the veins and interstices of things. Rather he is present in the things themselves. The stones of this church exist and are present by the continual effect of God's will. This body that I am, these feeling nerves, this beating heart, this vital breathing, continue and perform those rhythms of process by which my life persists, not of themselves alone, but as the perpetual expression of creative will. Let me pause and collect myself and quieten my busy thoughts, and feel in my own actual being the impress and expression of almighty Godhead. Each moment of my being, added to the last, is a further message to me, a soundless voice of the all-creative act. Let me feel, and listen, and receive in my own existence the bounty of God.

But now, to receive the effects of God's presence and power is still not to know God in himself. I see what comes out of the fountain: I cannot dive back into the hidden spring which is the divine life. Not, anyhow, so long as it is my body to which I attend. It is opaque, a dead end, I cannot look back through it into the power out of which its life constantly arises. Let me turn from my body, then, and think of my mind. And let me think, not of any and every state or act or thought, but rather of this present thought by which I am trying to know God. I have prayed God to guide and assist me, to show me himself: surely he has forgiven me my sins for Christ's sake; surely his goodness is actually here, supplying that thought by which I try to know him. I go on thinking, stringing words, shaping images. Where does all this come from? Out of a hidden depth of mental being, and down at the bottom of the well once more is God's creative power. My thought arises no less than my bodily existence out of the infinite reserves of God's will. O my God, let the waters that spring up be the waters of truth, let them arise out of your predestinating, prevenient grace, for otherwise they will be nothing worth. How can I think truly of You unless You give me the thought?

If, then, this rising fountain of my thought could be very clear and still, like a pool, could I look back into the depth of it, and see the open view in the rocky bottom out of which the living waters rise? How hard, among the stones, to mark and single out the crack from which the overflowing pool is born! But even if I can see it, I can see no further. Everything on this side is me, mine, my thought in its familiar quality and nature. God in the purity of God is all that is below, on the further side of that deep fissure. Even if I can see as far as the springing point, I have only reached the point of transformation at which God's creative act ends and my created action arises from it.

But now let me yield to fantasy. Let me suppose that I can borrow the nature of one of those thread-like transparent creatures of the water which seem only less liquid than the water itself. Let me suppose that I can dive into the vein of the spring and swim upwards against the current into the head of living waters, out of my thought into the will and mind of God.

Let me then swim and pass among those living waters which are life itself. Here I am amidst them where with scarcely moving weight they are passing towards the outlet up which I have come, the spring of my human mind. What are these waters? They are the divine will which underlies my will. Here I find, with penitence and amazement, my own thoughts, thought for me beforehand by God, in all the minuteness of their detail—nothing is too small for him to have forethought it: here are all my acts and ways. But how pure, how sweet, how clean they are in the predestinating grace of God. O my God, you have willed all this for me, and how I have muddled it with my sins! Here I find all the lovely archetypes of what my life has caricatured and distorted, and many noble, saving things so spoiled by me that their effects were never seen on my side, even to myself! O my God, clean out the passage of my fountain, let it be so no longer, O my God.

But let me swim still on beyond God's forethought of my thought and predestination of my ways into the very love from which they came, and explore that ocean of constant well-wishing and inexhaustible patience of mercy which overflows in all these divine intentions for my good. I will let this water flow over me and through me, to be joined with it, to share some part of your care, O God, for my friends and neighbours, yes, and for my own true good.

Can I go still further—can I come to the place from which the whole lake is filled, where a great cataract of waters flows soundlessly down and spreads without foam, falling from no cliff and issuing from no cavern, but constantly self-supplied as out of nothing, out of a bright clear air? God's being is sheer creation, he is all he wills to be, and wills to be all that he is.

But here I will shake myself from my dream, and repent my presumption. All this is vain fancy: what am I, to be able to explore the secrets of the divine abyss? I cannot dive through my fountain into you, O God, from whom I rise: I am condemned to remain here with myself. If there is any traffic between us it must be because you come through to me, not I to you. We cannot come to you, you are beyond our reach: but you can come to us, we are not beneath your mercy. With thee is the well of life, and in thy light we shall see light. The well of the mind is indeed dark, but is there not a thread of light, so fine that it is scarcely visible, rising at the bottom from the fissure of the spring? Let me be still, attend and watch, and see the lights gradually spread and extend, as the light of a candle does in a dark room into which we have newly entered: at first one sees nothing but the single thread of light upon the wick, but gradually the walls and features of the room lift themselves out of the darkness and are more and more clearly seen. So the dark well into which I am looking is mysteriously lighted from below, revealing—and this is wonderful—not the sides and bottom of the well itself, but other images. At first I see, of course, the reflections of what is above the well, perhaps the mass of my own head and shoulders looking down. But no, it is another face, and what is that on the head! I do not wear—no certainly I do not wear—a crown of thorns: sometimes you have given it me to wear, for a while, but I have always pulled it off and thrown it away. What is this pool? Is it not the magic mirror spoken of by St James, into which a man looking beholds the face of his new birth, the image of Christ which he is to be by grace, not the image of what sin grafted on nature has made him? Here is the mirror-image which forms the face that looks upon it, instead of being formed by that face. O my God, to think that I may thus look into myself, and see not that cursed reflection of my own vanity which haunts me, but the likeness of Christ which thou hast pre-destined me to wear! Can it be indeed that if I will faithfully medi-tate and be still, if I will give my thoughts to thee to shape and govern, thou wilt prefigure Christ in them?

But let me wake from this dream too. God, you are not present to me by any images, any pictures. All pictures lie, all images dis-tort. Why should I strive to figure and represent, when it has been said, Thou shalt not make a graven image? Is it not enough that you, more bright than any image, more full than any fountain, more alive than life itself, are actually here, feeding my soul with your grace? Let me be quiet while I can, and in naked faith receive him who is perfectly invisible, and clean outside my range of thought or power to conceive. What does it matter what I tell my-self? How am I the better for picture-making? You whom all pic-tures falsify are here.

And, last, from all dreams let me awake, and act. Do you only feed me while I think of it? Are you not my perpetual, my insepar-able, life? Let me thus go, and live out your inspirations. The best way to assure a constant supply is not to gaze into the bottom of the pool but to draw water out and scatter it on the garden, so as to make room for more to flow in below. Be with me, O God, and help me to obey thee in using and spreading abroad thy grace.

THE BELLS OF HEAVEN

I remember when I was an undergraduate, browsing about in books which were no proper concern of mine, coming across this phrase in a late mediaeval text: *ad septem horas de clocca*. If that was Latin, I was prepared to eat my hat; but Latin or not, it was the obvious original of our phrase: at seven o'clock. But how, I wondered, did it come, and what was a *clocca*, anyhow? A little research showed that *clocca* was a bell; and 'seven hours by the bell' may even go back to a time before mechanical clocks: someone being detailed to watch a sundial or an hour-glass, and pull the bell-rope in the steeple when the hour was up. Many of the early clocks were literally *cloccas*, i.e. time bells: interest was still centred on the bell, rather than the dial. I am the proud possessor of a seventeenth-century piece which I may well call a grandfather's clock, since it stood on my grandfather's stairs, as now it stands on mine. It has only one hand, and the face is hard to read; but the hour bell is so strong and clear, that it might wake the household, if we had not learned, with subconscious cunning, to discount it. But if we should lie awake, there it is, shattering the silence: one: one, two: one, two, three. Alas, the hours are overtaking us, and we are not getting our sleep. Or in the day—there's that bell already and I am still dawdling over my letters; my work is still untouched. The voices of bells impose on us the tyranny of an alien measure, measured to us by the revolutions of the earth through light and darkness. Left to ourselves, we should have our own rhythms, our own periodisations of life: the beating of our pulses, the cycle of hunger, search for food, eating, and round into hunger again; the cycle of curiosity, finding out, delight in discovery, peace of mind, and round to curiosity again. Such are the cycles which life makes for itself, measuring itself by its own rhythm. But no, it will not do, we are not content with these: we put ourselves under the tyranny of an alien measure, and force it upon our own consciousness by these accursed and accusing bells.

But if bells number our hours to us, we cannot really object, for our hours are numbered. I cannot hear the bell more than just so many times, as many as my seventy or so years allow: and then they will ring for me the bell which gives a shorthand or summary of all the bells I have heard, but shall hear no more; one stroke for every year of my life, counting me out, when I am dead. But meanwhile, here I am, alive, and how little use I make of the time which the bells ring away for me, hour upon hour.

The stroke of the hour bell makes us seem impotent and small, in face of the infinite and inexorable procession of measured time; makes us see our mortality and our guilt, as we fail to meet the challenge of the passing day. But not all bells humiliate us, by imposing on us an era not our own. There are bells which have the opposite effect. I remember the armistice day of the 1914 war, when sirens began to blow, and bells to ring. Those bells did not, like a conqueror's curfew, impose an alien time on us. The victory was a new era we ourselves had made. The steeples shook, the bells rent the air, as though to impose our achievement on the world. They did not tell us that we had been overtaken by an era, but that we had created one.

They did not tell us of time relentlessly pacing us, they suggested almost that time, war-time, that is, had ended: as for the peace which spread before us, it was not a race to be kept up with, but a liberty to be enjoyed. So when bells are rung to announce an heir to the throne: the royal mother hears the air humming with the new era to which her body has given birth. In former days, when the priest had consecrated the sacrament on the altar, they rang a bell, so that the busy people in the town might know that the sacramental presence had been once more vouchsafed, and so they might adore. And it is so with Christmas bells, Easter bells: they do indeed mark times and seasons, but their message is not that time has overtaken us, but that our salvation is born. They ring the bells when the bride comes out of church; and it must be a half-hearted bridegroom who reflects—time has overtaken me, my bachelor days are ended, and little I have to show for them. He has his bride to show, and that's enough: let everyone within sound of the steeple share the achievement, the glory.

A carol tells us that all the bells in heaven do ring on Christmas Day: and though it would be childishness to take such language for literal truth, yet symbolically speaking, it seems right. There are glories enough in heaven to rock the tallest steeples; our difficulty might be, to see why they should ever cease to sound, though they would not always please, nor even mean much, without intervening silences. But setting that aside—if marriage, if the consecration of the host are joys and achievements reaching on into eternity, what shall we say of that bridal day, which shall unite our souls for ever to the life of God, and to the company of the saints?

For the other sort of bell, the bell of time, cannot be thought, even by the most wayward and picturesque of poets, to toll in heaven. For, says St John, night there is none, there: no place, then, for bells, tolling out the divisions of day and night, where they have no use of lamplight or sunlight, even, for the Lord God lightens them; their lamp is the Lamb.

The thought of everlasting life often perplexes, or even dismays us: we think we are called upon to concern ourselves in a state where nothing happens, except that, perhaps, we feel ever more deeply, and understand ever more clearly. There is no warrant in Scripture, nor, I make bold to say, in right reason, for such a picture. Our immortality cannot be the timeless eternity of God, who infinitely transcends us; but an everlastingness suitable to our own nature, such as will permit us, while remaining ourselves to hang on the skirts of God's eternity, and drink the fountain of his peace. Nothing will *happen*, if you like—nothing befall us, or overtake us, like nightfall and the striking hour: we shall not run a race against the ebb of time. Nothing will happen to us passively, but much will be actively achieved: the life we shall draw from the Countenance we shall behold, will inspire us and carry us to splendid actions, glorious creations, happy partnerships: and why should not such works, brought to their perfection, merit the ringing of golden peals?

St John (i,5) says that Christ is a light in the darkness of this world, a light which the darkness never overtook—not, I think, never *comprehended*, as our old version has it: that is not the point in this place. In a sense, Christ was as much overtaken as any of us, by nightfall and the striking hour. Very often, we must suppose, since he was the type of that good Samaritan, who turned aside from his scheduled journeys to heed the cry of need. Darkness overtook him, he fell short of his inn, and camped by the wayside. And yet, it did not *overtake* him, as an alien thing: for he was himself, says St John, the Word by whom the world was made, and through whom light and darkness were both appointed. He was no more *overtaken* by the darkness, than I am *overtaken* by the words I freely speak. His earthly mission, his charitable action, were one with the cycles of the sun and moon; they all went together to compose the single but manifold purpose of God. He did not fret at the passage of time, it did not accuse him of negligence, nor did it mock him for his impotence. He had taught, he had healed, he had journeyed, he had prayed as the time allowed. That his planned journey should fail, all this was carried in the higher plan by which, human choice and heavenly providence concurring, he moved forward to the redemption of mankind, and the marriage of heaven with earth. He never watched time running through his fingers: when he still had more than thirty years in hand, he spent them at a single throw, and bought the pearl of infinite price. You can say that, in the end, he embraced darkness: he never let it overtake him.

When I was a boy, my father, wishing to encourage me at once in Greek and in handicraft, and to edify himself at the same time, caused me to carve him a little wooden plaque, with the words, *ERCHETAI NUX*, night cometh; the night, that is, in which no man can work. And this he put under the clock in his study, to discourage him from idleness, a warning, it seems to me, he of all men least needed; and yet, when he came to the end of his life, he would lament how little he had made of it. And so we are all likely to feel. Time accuses us, time, and those awful words, 'We have left undone what we ought to have done'—for God knows what that is. And when we are most triumphant in the sense of having overtaken time, and imposed our achievement on the day, we may have most cause to rue, in our supposed success, the failure to have done the only thing that would have been truly worth while.

If we have to suppose that any souls are condemned to everlasting misery, surely a striking clock will not be left out of the equipment of their prison; the sound of time relentlessly passing, and never occupied to the hearer's content. A life on earth continually overtaken by time, and by remorse, is a pattern of damnation: but if we suffer such a hell on earth, it is only for lack of taking hold upon the redemption so freely offered to us. The Light, which darkness overtaketh not has shined on our heads: he who commits his soul to Christ is one with the will which made both night and day. He puts himself into the hands of Christ, to live in his will. He will not be perfect, and so he will have many repentances for time misspent; but he will be humble and believing, therefore he will feel no remorse.

He will say: I missed this or that call from a fellow-being, I followed my pride, or my pleasure, I did not do as you, my Lord, would have done. But you have let me fall into these errors to show me my heart, and you, in your mercy, will use them for my discipline, and turn them to account in the designs of your loving kindness. You have undertaken my life, and you will bring it to good. While we are yours, we shall never be overtaken by darkness; work out in us the purpose of your perfect will and bring us to that day, which will marry us to joy, and ring every peal in all the city of heaven.

THE DAY'S WORK

Family faces was a great game with my aunts. We, their unfortunate nephews and nieces, had to submit to have our features dissected, and given away to various relations we had barely heard of. My nose was not mine, it was great uncle George's nose. My right eyebrow (a bad match to my left) was the property of cousin Hannah Maria — though she was so collateral, it was a puzzle to see how her eyebrow had got on to my head. My aunts might disagree about the true attribution of my several bits and pieces, the one thing they agreed upon, was that none of it was mine — I was a ragshop of patches, I was synthetic to the last drop.

I have heard the same game played with the masterpieces of literature, and even taken a hand in the game myself. St John's Gospel, now, that is a favourite subject for dissection. He got his ideas from the Jewish rabbis — he got them from Greek mystical philosophers — he got them from a sect of half-Christian theosophists — not a bit of it; he got them from the Essenes who wrote the scrolls they dug up by the Dead Sea. The one thing nobody suspects him of having done is think for himself, or turn his eye upon the facts he was attempting to report. But then one listens to a piece like this ninth chapter we have just read, one meets the realism, the shattering force and practicality of it, and one wonders what one has been dreaming of. Here is no repetition of borrowed ideas — indeed, here are no ideas at all, there is just a fact: Jesus heals the blind. The ideas in the chapter are all irrelevances, pushed in by people who cannot face the impact of facts, but cloud them over with words and theories.

The disciples begin it. Here is a man born blind. They want to theorise: Jesus means to act. Was the blindness a punishment for the sins God foresaw the man would commit, or for the sins his parents committed? Jesus says that the blindness is not to be thought of as the effect of guilt, but as the opportunity of grace. It will serve to show the saving love of God. Jesus does not mean that God made the man blind on purpose, so as to have the glory of healing him. What could be more childish? It is more like this—the disciples are trying to relate the man's blindness to the will of God by presumptuous speculations on guilt and punishment. No, says Jesus: this is the way to relate it to the will of God—and he steps forward to heal. Life is too short for such speculation. We must work (says Jesus) the works of the Father who sent me, while it is day: the night cometh when no man can work. While I am in the world, I am the light of the world.

The man is no sooner healed, than fresh ideas are brought in to cloud the issue. The blind cannot now be seeing. There is a confusion of persons. The blind man and the seeing man are different men. And then again: he cannot really be healed, because they cannot understand the method employed, or see why it should work. And then another line of objection—and this is worst of all—Jesus cannot have healed him, for Jesus is not Orthodox. Jesus has preferred to heal a sufferer, rather than to keep the Sabbath. Admittedly the man has recovered—it is the inexplicable act of God—but Jesus really had nothing to do with it. In a sense, Jesus agrees. Jesus has no claim and no wish to add anything to the work of God—it cannot be better than divine: he sinks himself in the action of his Father in heaven. But he does sink himself in it: the act of healing is divinely good, Sabbath or no Sabbath. Jesus and his Father are one. If they cannot see that the very thing he is doing is heavenly, then what can they know of God?

Is not God the very Father of light? Uncountable ages (as we now know) before there was an eye to see, light irradiated the field of space, pouring from every star; and the old biblical story, which spanned the whole creative work in the compass of a week, made the creation of light the morning of the first, and the creation of man the evening of the last creative day. So late it was that man came into his inheritance; man, the child of light: for does not man's mind swim in light, as fishes in water, or birds in air? It is true that we have five different senses: but touch and taste reach no further than the organs they employ, smell samples our immediate atmosphere, and sound gives few clear informative reports beyond a range of fifty yards. But sight travels out and back along the paths of light and plots the compass of the universe. Our other senses are chiefly concerned with our fellow-creatures, our food, and our material pleasures. Sight shows us a world of things with calm objectivity, in their own colours and their mutual relations; sight gives us some clue to the survey of that all-seeing eye, which is in truth no eye at all, but the unspotted mirror of an infinite mind, where all things, as well invisible to us as visible, are perfectly discerned and individually loved.

Other creatures beside ourselves have sight, we alone have the mind to enter into our visual inheritance; and though it is truly said that thinking goes beyond seeing, yet it is no mean glory of our mind, or ignoble measure of our scope, that it can stretch to cover the field of light which vision opens to us.

Why, then, if we unlock the doors of darkness, and admit a blind man to the world of sight, is not the work divine? Surely there is no argument; whether it is done by prayer and miracle, or by surgery and skill. I was hearing the other day of a man who, by a sudden infection of his only seeing-organ, went blind in a minute. He could not believe his change; he opened his lids and strained his eyeballs, he groped for the switch and turned on light, but still there was nothing. Imagine it! Or think of the opposite—in our own time living lenses have been grafted on defective eyes, and those who never saw from the day of their birth have, in their grown manhood, possessed the universe of light.

Sight teaches objectivity of view, and steady, appreciative contemplation; we forget ourselves, set aside our prejudices, and let the thing seen passively instruct us. Such is the lesson of light, and yet the lesson is not learnt. The ninth chapter of St John is a sad reflection on human perversity. A man sees: and they will not see it. And so they condemn themselves as blind. For judgement came I into this world, that they which see not may see; and that they which see may become blind, says Christ.

What a reflection on human perversity, and what a rebuke to the Christian disunion, which we are called upon to repent today. Instead of recognising the work of God where they saw it, the Pharisees applied the test of formal rules. Christ broke the Sabbath. He was no disciple of Moses in the true succession. What example could apply more exactly to the attitude of Christians to those divided from them by empirical allegiance! He is not sound on Biblical Inspiration. He is incorrect on the doctrine of Justification by faith alone. He is outside legitimate Catholic order. And all these things may have their place: but the first thing is the acknowledgement of the work of Christ, wherever it is manifested, in healing sores and making saints. It is divine, it cannot be gainsaid. What can God himself do with us if we will not love, and welcome, and assist the manifest work of God? We can, in the end, commend the doctrines and institutions of religion by nothing else but this, that they are channels appointed to convey, and actually conveying, the efficacious grace of Christ.

The spirit of faction, and of that self-hatred which is the twin of self-righteousness, can so bedevil religion as to make it a form of positive evil, and a blinding of the heart. Where is the man who will see things as they are and allow God to instruct his mind through an unbiased appreciation? He is the man without an axe to grind; and the first thing the world sees in religious believers, is that they are the grinders of axes. They dare not take things as they come, or see things as they are, for fear of disturbing their prejudices or cherished beliefs.

Who can say, surveying the field of history, whether religion, yea, and even professed Christianity, has been a greater cause of blindness and rancour than of charity and vision? I do not think the historical case is worth fighting. But then spiritual truth was never known by counting heads: the saints are our instructors. And it is still true, that the best way to see and to love the work of God in all this world of his is to look for it, and when we see it, to adore. And this, true religion does.

Christ said of the blind man, that his misfortune was an occasion for the word of God to be manifested in him; and that they (that is, Jesus and his disciples) must work at God's work, while the daylight held. How I wish that, every time I am confronted with another man's trouble, or another man's faithlessness I could remember this truth! It is not something for me to be disturbed by, or discouraged by, still less, annoyed or grieved by. It is an opportunity the heart of God covets, to do his loving work: and he has appointed me, with whatever capacity I have, to be his instrument. So, heaven help me! But the case is really the same, is it not, when I am met by my own faults of character and temper, my failures in religion or in work: a heavenly opportunity for the grace of God! I am not to grieve over old miseries, but submit myself to those healing hands, and give the healer the joy for which he longs.

Above all, we are blind: blindfold in our prejudice, blinkered by our preoccupations, drugged in our self regard: we do not see the glory of God. And above all, God longs to open our eyes. Here at

least we know what the cure is. All we have to do is to practise looking through the eyes of Christ: and this is the contemplative part of
prayer, when, invoking his aid, we turn over quietly what we know
of God or have just read in the scriptures, and try to see our lives
and our neighbours in the light of it, and, what we have seen, to
love and to adore.

IVORY TOWERS

—preached in Keble College Chapel, St Luke's Day, 1965

The dons (as you may guess) have their own little games. Among these games is the propounding of learned riddles. A couple of terms ago the Fellows of Keble were passing round the question, why *ivory tower*? Why do they say that we academics are shut in an *ivory tower* when they mean that we make ourselves remote, and wash our hands of the workaday world? The question was passed to and fro amongst us: it was never satisfactorily answered. We traced the phrase as far as a mid-nineteenth century French poet; but when we asked what he was alluding to in choosing the image, we reached no certain conclusion.

I am afraid that the indignant journalists who bombard our ivory towers would have felt that our little learned game was just so much more evidence for the truth of their accusation. What could be more ivory-towerish than to trifle in this way? You accuse men of sitting in ivory towers, and instead of taking it to heart, and trying to get out, they turn the question into an ivory tower game. So deeply ingrained is their instinct for ivory towersmanship.

People all over the place, one finds, are haunted by a sense of not being in the real world, and so of not being quite real themselves: as though we had to pinch ourselves to make sure we were really there. Somewhere outside our magic garden, we feel convinced something called real life is going on; and so we make occasional raids on the great Outside, looking for Life with a big L. Undergraduates think it is terribly unreal or artificial to be living on grants. Real life means earning money: so we take a job in the vacation, sorting letters at the post office. How real is that, though? A boring, routine occupation, concerned with the outsides of letters; letters mostly about nothing real, even if you opened them.

Though, at your age, I suppose I knew I was a predestined academic, I went in pursuit of Reality into a provincial town curacy. And what did I find? A widening of experience, certainly, but I assure you, a plentiful crop of unrealities among the more satisfying fruits; and when in due course I submitted to doing what I seemed made for, and returned to the University, I did not find a loss of reality in the change.

There is life everywhere to be lived, if we will only live it, yet everywhere the sense of unreality haunts us . . .

But look here, ought not I to stop moaning like this, and talk to you about St Luke? Dear St Luke! What a charming and gentle, and civilised, and Greek impression he makes, compared with all these fierce, uncompromising Israelites who wrote us our Bible! If *he* cannot win us to the love of God, who can? Yet I do not find that I can know St Luke. He wrote his books, God bless him; he did not talk about himself. I shall not talk about him either, I shall talk more in general about what a saint is; and we have access to a host of saints whom we can see into much better than we can into St Luke. When I fall victim to that haunting sense of unreality which besets us all, I call on a man who spends his life in a much better way than I do, and I say to him, 'Dig me out a saint.' So he goes to the library, and finds me one. A saint: a saint portrayed by his contemporaries, and expressed in his own recorded words.

Now I dare say that to many people a saint means someone 'quite out of this world', but I can only record my experience, that the characteristic of the saint is to be massively real. True it is, that none but God himself is entitled to say 'I am what I am'. It would seem blasphemous to say that there is no nonsense about the divine nature; but if it is blasphemous, it is merely because it so obviously doesn't need saying, that to say it is an impertinence. God first is; but as for us, we have to make ourselves, if we are ever going to be anything worth having. And so we must always wonder whether what we are making of ourselves isn't a pose, or some sort of a sham. And so there is a certain element of nonsense about all of us; we cannot take ourselves or one another too seriously: we are not what we are.

It is easy to say, 'Be yourself', if you could find the self you are supposed to be: but what is it? Some people think that they are being themselves, and wonderfully sincere, if they identify themselves with their worst and most primitive passions. But that is to be little better than an animal, and how can I be myself by being a beast? I am a man, surely, and how can I be myself by forgetting my noblest part? Where is the sincerity in a man's being a beast? Yet if I attempt to follow a higher ideal of myself, how easily do I become a prig or a hypocrite.

The saint has solved the problem of sincerity in the sole possible way by turning to God, the great I AM, and accepting the self his creator designed for him. And the quest of the self God has meant each of us to be is like the quest of happiness (which is indeed much the same thing)—it is not found by looking for it. We do not ask of God, 'What sort of person did you mean me to be?'—we say to him 'Lord, what wilt thou have me to do?'

Without the living and constant service of the divine will, religion can be nothing but a delusion. We find our true being by letting God make us what he would have us; and this he does by directing our particular actions, day by day.

I mentioned just now my far too rare excursions into the lives of the saints. The last saint my wise friend dug out for me was St Vincent de Paul, a Frenchman contemporary with our Charles I. He is remembered by his grateful country, because in conditions of appalling squalor and distress he organised Sisters of Charity to go into the homes of the poor and to combat the plague. But he was not only a philanthropist: he was a saint. You can still read the verbatim account of the discussion-classes he held with these sisters. They were rough young peasant-girls, for he had decided that the pious ladies of Paris would never stand the racket. These girls had to be taught their a.b.c.: and he gave them classes in prayer. We can still read their artless remarks, and his always positive and encouraging replies.

'What do you do when you pray?' he asked them. 'Father,' a girl replied, 'I listen to God.'—'You could not do better,' he said, 'only would it not be more correct to say, you listen for God? You put yourself in his presence, and you take up an attitude of devout attention. That is all you can do. But God will make you aware, as it pleases him, of what he means you to know concerning his will.' Prayer, he said, that does not issue in practical resolutions is a delusion: and the resolutions should commonly bear on your duty for the day. So the saint and his band of workers *found* God by meditating in the scenes of Christ's life. They listened for his will in the direction of their duty. They went out, and they did it in ministry to the sick or the poor. They made faults, of course. They were frightened or they were cross. They came back in humility to their prayers, received their fresh directions and inspiration, and went out again to their work.

This happy circle of praying and living surely banished unreality as effectively as it can be banished in this life. There was no humbug about God. Their God was the love which controlled them, and whom they obeyed: they knew him as a horse knows his rider, by the hand on the reins. There was no humbug about themselves either; for they were wholly occupied in doing what they knew they must do; and they became what their God-given lives made of them. They had no time for studying their personalities in any mental looking-glass: they saw themselves only in the eyes of the poor, and in the eyes of their God.

Well, no such a privilege of calling has come to us. I suppose it is right that God desires most men to follow the decent and humdrum occupations we propose to follow, or how is the world to go on? And for the present we are in this University. Let us accept that God means us to be here, but let us go on to see how he means us to live here. We shall never know God unless we listen for him, and let him direct us. He will tell us very simple things, and he will tell us them again and again: to make a proper job of our work—to go out of our way to be encouraging to dull and discouraged people— to control our lustful hearts—to manage our lives sensibly, so that we can sleep, communicate and pray—to live with our friends for their pleasure, not for our own glory: to do important things first and attractive things second. God will teach us these simple lessons again and again. He will also bring into our minds particular duties, and make us see particular needs. There is no religion, and no escape from unreality, without God's will.

But perhaps it is not all God asks of us, to be faithful in our present station. Since we spare so much time for recreation, perhaps he asks us to spare a little for something more in the line of what St Vincent and his helpers did. There are hospitals to be visited, lonely and housebound old people to be befriended, jobs of manual work to be done for those who cannot themselves do them. The doing or not doing of such things, like every other decision, should be referred to the will of God. How can I best use my time in this world? That is our question before the face of God. One day we shall have eternity to play with, but now we've only got time, and it's a perishing commodity. Let us receive it and use it as from the hands of God.

THE UNDYING FIRE

—preached in Trinity College Chapel, Oxford, October 1959

What do you think of the Election? Without taking sides, we may
agree that it's hard cheese on the Labour Party. The measures they
took in 1945 have turned half the proletariat into a petite bour-
geoisie; and now these ungrateful people vote for the bourgeois side.
The Conservatives, as befits them, put an amiable complexion on
the matter; it shows, they say, that the class-war is obsolete. But it
is always easy to alter the moral assessment of political facts; and it
is possible to put things in a way less flattering to the electoral
majority. Not, they have seen through the class-war; but that,
admitted to the charmed circle of privilege, they don't mean to see
it more widely extended. We are most of us very comfortable here;
while admittedly three-quarters of the world is on the verge of mal-
nutrition. Ah, but would the Socialists do any more than the Conservatives for hungry men with dusky hides? I don't pretend to say
—I don't suppose we should let them, even if they wanted to. The
great mass of men will not support a crusade against misery, unless
they feel the pinch. When they do feel it, though—and this is surprising—something more than selfishness often comes in. Common
distress produces common sympathy: there is something genuine
and charitable, while it lasts, about the crusading spirit of revolu-
tionary parties.

Here we are, you see, you and I, sitting on the splendid altitudes
of our moral elevation, and passing an Olympian judgement on the
motives of mankind. Poor beasts, we no sooner rid them of their
oppressions, than they turn into a herd of complaisant materialists.
So we say, as though we were quite uninvolved in the situation we
are discussing; but aren't we involved? And have we the right to
talk? We are all drawing benefits from the welfare-state, just as
much as any factory-worker, or old age pensioner. The University
and its members are all subsidised directly or indirectly, in some
half-dozen different ways. The system defends our study and
assures our leisure; moreover it makes us tolerably certain of suit-

able employment afterwards, without our greatly exerting ourselves. The temptation to nestle down and suck the sweets of our situation is nowhere stronger than it is in this University (and—dare I add—in this College): the old hands will hardly dispute what I say, and you who are new to the life will soon discover it.

But you aren't middle-aged yet, thank heaven, so there's still hope of you; you aren't yet irredeemably corrupted. Somewhere in your hearts, however buried under piles of worldly rubbish, there smoulders the embers of a divine discontent: you mean to burn yourself out one of these days in a blaze of glory. Let others wallow in their material lot, but you will not—or only for a while: you are just taking a little moral holiday, collecting your strength and choosing your objective; and then you'll show them, yes, you'll show them. For somewhere, hidden in the nooks and corners of the world, waiting to be unearthed, there is your thing: something to possess you, and kindle you, and burn you out in seventy years—you'll write, you'll discover, you'll govern, you'll acquire, you'll entertain—what shall it be? Perhaps even—perhaps you'll be a heroic social benefactor, and forget your own concerns in healing the plagues or sorrows of unhappy men. Is there not such a dream somewhere in everyone's mind—a compensation, a glorious what-I-shall-be, to distract attention from the ignoble what-I-am?

Moses, the disillusioned exile, feeding a foreigner's sheep, saw a blaze of fire burning in a bush, only that the bush was not consumed. A voice sounded in his mind: 'I am the God of thy fathers; I will send thee to bring forth my people, the Children of Israel, out of Egypt': as though he had said, I am the fire that will kindle you; my will and my life shall set you ablaze, to make you a saviour and a prophet.

Yet God did not, according to the story, call Moses there and then to approach, to step into the divine fire and be set alight. He said, 'Draw not nigh hither; set thy shoes from off thy foot: the place thou treadest is holy ground.' It seemed impossible to the ancient people, that man should blaze in the fire of God, and not be destroyed. 'Who,' they said, 'shall see God, and live? How shall we dwell with everlasting burnings?' And yet the sign God showed to Moses held the promise of this very thing: the bush burned, and was not consumed. The fire of God was to blaze in the tree of Israel which he had planted, and the tree would flourish, as though the flames were sunlight, and the heat was dew.

Moses built a tabernacle in the midst of the camp, and Solomon a temple in the city of Zion. They fenced round a holy space, they set a great altar in the midst of it. They piled the wood, and laid the offering; and (such was Israel's belief) the lightning fell, and God came down in fire. Kindled by heaven above, the pillar of flame went up, and there, day and night, they nourished it: you saw it burning from afar, as you drew near to Zion. There was the fire of God, the place of sacrifice; and though the Israelite could not throw himself into it, he could throw in the offering, the choice of his possessions, standing for himself, and given to God. The blue smoke twisted skywards, and he had fellowship with Glory.

But the fellowship must be more close: the fire must catch us. We are all in the place of Moses, and a voice speaks to us suddenly out of solitude: I am the God of your Fathers—I have heard the cry of my people, and I have come down. We look, and we see a fire of the divine glory, burning in a sweet flourishing tree, which is not consumed—that is, we see Jesus, a kind face of human flesh, in which the very godhead burns; and yet his common manhood is not destroyed. It is all the more natural, all the more enduring for the life and love of God which glows through it. Unlike the apparition of God which spoke to Moses, Christ does not say to you, 'Stand back, the place is holy: put the shoes from off your feet'; he says, 'Come here to me, all that labour or carry burdens, and I will give you rest.' He invites us to step into his flame, to kindle at it, and so to have our hearts' desire.

As I was saying, we all look round, in our more exalted moments, for something to kindle us, some fire of noble action in which to burn the fuel of our life, before it rots. But we have only to take one step out of ourselves, and we shall stand in the magic fire, the fire of Christ. Who knows indeed how high a part, or how humble, we may be called to play? But we have not, in any case, to kindle our own fire, or fan it with the breath of our own lips. 'I have come to cast fire upon earth,' said Jesus; and that fire is enough to enflame us. We have only to accept our place in Christ's body, to become instruments of a will we know, and channels of a life that we have received. What higher glory is there? What do we wait for any longer? Today if ye will hear his voice, harden not your hearts.

That Christ is the green tree burning and unconsumed, and the ultimate meaning of Moses's vision, what Christian can doubt? For first, the divine fire coming down on Mary left her the woman she was, and made her son, like any of us, a laughing, crying child. Then the divine life growing with the growth of Jesus, and carrying him to heights of heroic love, put no strain on his humanity. Constantly burnt away in sacrifice to his Father and his friends, he became all the more the dear man that he was: his flesh was warm, because his Spirit was divine. And last, when the flames of sacrifice wrapped him round, and, to all common reckoning, consumed him utterly, for he died, then, by a supreme glory and outbreak of the life of God, then he was alive among his friends, the tree burning and unconsumed. His eyes, says St John, were like a flame of fire; his feet like burnished brass, smelted in a furnace; his countenance was as the sun shines in his strength. When I saw him, I fell at his feet, as dead. But he laid his hand upon me, saying: Fear not: I am the Living who was dead, and behold, I am alive for evermore.

The image is more evident in some of Christ's martyrs, who passed the literal ordeal of fire, by the strength he gave them. Thus fire conquered fire, the fire of Christ the flame of the scaffold; as, in the old Latin hymn the martyr says to his executioner:

> The tree afire and yet entire
> Defeats the brands your godless hands
> Heap hither, halbardier.
> *Ignis urens non conburens*
> *Vincit prunas quas adunas*
> *O minister impie.*

But Christ also, like Solomon, has founded an altar where the flame of his sacrificial love always burns; and so at this season Christendom gives thanks for its Churches, and we for our chapel in the feast of dedication, because here at this altar we can return again and again, week by week, to throw ourselves back into the living sacrifice of Christ, the joy and the glory. And though to our now remorseful eyes it seems that we learn nothing of Christ and do little but grieve the Holy Ghost, between one communion and another; yet our saviour is more generous far than we, or why did he die? He knows what he has given us, and in his eyes a grain of love outweighs a world of folly. And he will teach us to be Christians not ancient Jews, and to say with delight, and not with fear, OUR GOD IS A CONSUMING FIRE.

THE MINGLING WATERS

—preached in Trinity College Chapel, Oxford, 1960

In spite of all that industry has done to the city, for good or evil, in spite of the clutter of parked cars, or the menace of moving traffic, it warms the heart of middle-age to observe how, at the beginning of term, undergraduates treat the whole town as if it were one vast quad and shout their uninhibited greetings to one another across the street, between one omnibus and another; as unconcernedly as they did in those happy days, when so much grass grew in the High Street, during vacation, they put in sheep to nibble it down and make way for the tandems and dogcarts of gentlemen commoners. Love will find out a way, as the poet observed; and so will friendship, even between a Bedford truck and a vintage Bentley.

There is good old John, always good, but even better after six weeks' absence. There is no doubt that, meeting our friends after such an interval, we find that they have sorted themselves out into two collections; those whose presence causes our bosoms to dilate, and those who have no such effect on our vital being. We will neglect for the moment the second and less interesting group of specimens, and concentrate on the objects of our warmer enthusiasm. The great merit of these persons is, that not content with being enjoyable, they enjoy us. Our tutor greets us with an equivocal smile. There is a certain irony in his enquiries about the way we have spent our vacation. He does not take us on trust, he proposes collection-papers; but our friends, they accept us. They do not want us to be different. Even in our parents' farewell, there was an undercurrent, though unexpressed, of mind-you-are-a-good-boy-and-make-good-use-of-your-time. But with our friends, there is no question of raising the level to the proper height before we can open the water-gates. They are always open. Our minds run freely in and out through one another. The touch of friendship is the touch of life; our friends feed our very being.

When apostolic writers talk to us about fellowship, or communion, this is the sort of thing they are talking about. Life has to be shared, or it doesn't even live. Not even in God himself. The persons of the Blessed Trinity are each life, and God, to one another. There is nothing better anyone can offer us, than free fellowship. St John, in the beginning of his first epistle, tells his readers that life has been manifested, eternal life; it has been put in trust with the Apostles. They preach, but they do not merely preach, for preaching is not enough. Life must be communicated through fellowship. What we have seen and heard, we declare to you, he says, and why? Not simply that you may know it, but that you may have fellowship with us: and the effect of the fellowship will be the usual one—that our happiness, he says, may be complete: and so, you see, it is the real thing.

Yes, the real thing, and more real than that. For, he says, 'We write, that you may have fellowship with us; and indeed our fellowship is with the Father, and with his Son, Jesus Christ.' And there's the heart of the mystery: a fellowship with human friends, which is to be at the same time a fellowship with the Persons of the Godhead.

I suppose that you and I, left to ourselves, would be inclined to say something like this. As we've been recalling, there's friendship on earth. That's easy, or anyhow, not very hard. It comes naturally when you've found the right person. But then there's friendship with heaven. That's another thing. One would have to look for it in one's prayers. But prayer to us is little more than the ceremony of friendship: by using the forms of conversation we give body to a faith in the invisible, rather than to a fellowship with the present Christ. We know that mystical saints, making a life-work of it, going through agonies of exercise and deserts of dereliction, found an unearthly state of union with God. And we know that some of our friends, without any of these mystical pretentions, speak of having a talk with the Saviour of the world: but we find that all they mean is reading his words in the Gospel, and telling him what they think about it. And so we are baffled, or held up, at the essential step in achieving true religion: we ought to have fellowship with God, as we do with men, and we can't achieve it.

If that is your predicament, then you have every reason for attending with great care to what St John says: for he promises you a way out. It is quite untrue, according to him, that fellowship with man, and fellowship with God, are poles apart. They can be brought to coincide. Not all fellowship with men is fellowship with God: it may be a conspiracy in crime, more likely still in vanity and idleness.

But St John, at least, and his fellow-disciples, who have heard and seen and handled the Word of Life, they offer a fellowship to their friends, which is also a fellowship with the Father and the Son.

How can this be? Let us spend the next few minutes probing a little into the mystery. And let us begin by going back to what we were saying about friendship. Our friends are those who accept us, who approve of us. In their company we, who doubt so much of ourselves, cease to doubt. We are taken back into the great lap of life. This is peace. And yet it is not the deepest peace. We are approved of—that is something—but are we approved of *by the truth itself*? Is there not too much complacency here, too much indulgence? Does the approval of our friends confirm us in our self-regard, our frivolity of mind, our laziness? It may even worry us to see them so much pleased with our worst jokes.

But perhaps there is somewhere a kind bosom on which you can repose, where to be accepted is to be accepted by the truth itself; for there beats the heart of a Christian, even of a saint. There was a time—it is only a matter of going far enough back in memory, and we shall reach it—when our parent, fallible being though he or she may be, was the living truth for us; embodied all the moral light our elementary self was capable of seeing. To be accepted, or approved, by that dear person was to rest on the bosom of the truth itself, to be in union with God.

Perhaps that is one reason why God is above all named our Father, that he is the person in whom love and truth coincide. We outgrow our earthly Father, and begin a pilgrimage in search of the heavenly. St John and his fellow disciples found what they sought in the Son of the Father, his true representative and image; accepted by Jesus Christ in free companionship, they knew that they were in the truth, for he was truth itself.

But when St John wrote his letter, Jesus had been more than half a century dead, risen, ascended. One could not find in his visible and human companionship the union of truth and love. Therefore it is that St John offers the companionship of Christians: 'Have fellowship,' he says, 'with us: and our fellowship, indeed, is with the Father, and with his Son Jesus Christ.'

But how can it be, that basking in the kindness of Christ's disciples, they are to be rejoicing in the heart of God? Jesus was the truth: if you were accepted by him, you were loved by the truth itself. Is St John, is St Peter or any disciple, truth itself?

No. But St John goes on to explain how faulty men can be the deputies of the truth, so that in having fellowship with them, we may have fellowship with truth. They must be sincere: they must put themselves under the truth. Sincerity, says St John, has two branches. The first is a genuine endeavour to do all the will of God we know. 'If we say we have fellowship with the God of light, and walk in the darkness, we lie, and do not the truth.' But we are equally insincere if we fail to confess our transgressions against the light we obey. 'If we say we have no sin, we deceive ourselves, and the truth is not in us.'

Our friends, then, are to see the Christ in us, and we in them, first, as a power and a life moving us to practical goodness and honest speech: second, as a light which judges our dark patches, and a mercy that forgives us our sins.

It seems an odd ceremony, when Christians with one voice confess in general the sins they cannot in public particularise, and receive a general absolution. Yet, if we are to believe St John, this is nothing but the expression of a most happy avowal which makes us all fit to mediate to one another the fellowship of Christ. We submit to his law, with sincere intent, but we disown all pretence of perfection. So the light of his truth, and the warmth of his forgiveness can radiate through each of us to every other.

What it all amounts to is this. Christians do not need to be perfect, before they can find in one another an acceptance and an approval which is that of the truth itself; or rather, let us say, the truth himself, Jesus Christ. For the standard of truth will be there, alive in us, and judging us: the Spirit and the mind of Christ will be there in our standards, our attitudes, in our love of others' goodness, and our disowning of our own baseness.

There can be a Christian Society, when the mind of Christ reigns in inspiration and in judgement and in forgiveness: and those who have fellowship in it have fellowship with the Father and the Son. And if we are far from such a practical truth, we are to remember that, however falsified in us, it remains true in him. The living truth is there, for Christ is always there: and at any moment we can step back into the paradise of truth which we have lost, by returning to him. Not only will he reconcile us to himself: he will enable us to mediate his truth in unaffected friendship with one another, and in the faces of Christians to meet their master's eyes.

THE WINDOW INTO HEAVEN

On making a Retreat
—preached in Keble College Chapel, 1965

At this morning's Mattins, at eight o'clock, in the presence of a highly select audience, there was read the First Chapter of Genesis; and this evening before a not exactly populous, but still more numerous attendance, the Second Chapter has been recited. Now in the view of those who taught me divinity, the thing is to be deplored—deplored, I mean, that fewer ears should have received the first chapter than received the second. For my teachers held that the first chapter was better stuff—better, because later, and more developed. The second chapter, they said, is childish, with its picture of God moulding a gardener for his paradise out of clay, like a toddler playing with plasticine; and then bringing him alive by blowing breath into his nostrils. How much more philosophical the later scribe who added the first chapter. He took a much more grown-up view: he saw that the Almighty can make everything by the mere word of his power, that is, by the mere resolve of his will.

So said my teachers, but I didn't agree with them and still I don't. The history of religion doesn't go up and up and up, like the history of science, or like those terrible elevators in the new engineering laboratory that never stop elevating. Often, in religion, there's something in the earlier and discarded images which goes straight to one's heart; and I could not accept the great executive deity, who does everything just by giving orders, in place of that dear God whose fingers are on our clay and whose breath is in our nostrils; and who, when he has made us, comes to walk with us in the orchard-paths of his paradise.

Religion did not go up and up in bible-times, and neither does it in ours. Though nowadays we have got something which does not even pretend to be progress, it's simply fashion. You must be switched-in to the current wave-length, that's about all there is to it. And no doubt, childish as we are, God studies us, and means that we should keep our interest alive by hunting spiritual trails all together, like a pack of hounds. So now we are all in full cry after common action, togetherness—ecumenism on the grand scale and liturgical worship on the small scale; and personal religion is at a discount. To show how far the wheel has turned in a generation, I need only recall the most quoted and admired saying of the twenties and thirties, 'Religion is what a man does with his solitude.' Only think of it! With his solitude! The great Professor Whitehead couldn't have got away with that remark today.

Or could he? What do you think? Perhaps the wheel is turning again, and Whitehead's crashing aphorism might come home to some of you with the force of a new discovery. Someone says to me, What does religion amount to, anyhow? We have heartening (or sometimes not all that heartening) common ceremonies, by which we commit ourselves to certain social attitudes. We say we are giving ourselves *en masse* to the will of God, but what does the will of God amount to, when you look at it, but behaving amicably to our neighbours? The medicine works, not to a striking, but still to a perceptible extent—by and large, practising Christians are slightly more dependable, socially, than the rest of the population. So perhaps, on balance, Religion is a Good Thing. But where does God come into it? Isn't it all a pious fable, that Religion is primarily concerned with God? Are his fingers on our clay, moulding us? Do we draw life from the breath of his lips? Does he visit our orchard in the cool of the evening? Does any real experience correspond to such figures of speech?

Well, try a bit of solitude. Every now and then, but never often enough, I make what is called a retreat. The essence of the thing is not what one does, but what one doesn't. It does not greatly matter what one reads or what plan of spiritual performances, if any, one follows. What is essential is to make an artificial break with one's common existence, and to stop all the ploys, worthy or unworthy, that fill one's daily life. It is a patch of silence; a contrived vacuum. When you've emptied everything out, what is there? What is there which, try as you may, you can't empty out? There's God.

To make a retreat, then, is just to make a practical act of faith. If God is really everywhere, then if we clear a space, he'll still be there —or will he? Again and again the poor weak-hearted Christian is struck with the *horror vacui*, the terror of emptiness: if I make a gap in the fuss of living, it will be death to the spirits, vacancy to the mind, ice in the heart. Even so, very ordinary Christians manage to make a retreat sometimes; it's an act of faith, though the faith it springs from is no more than a grain of mustard-seed, as Jesus said — but even that amount of faith suffices to remove mountains.

Well, and what can we promise you? Ecstasies, visions, feelings of presence? Nothing like it: only the force of Living Truth. If I may jump back a minute. We were considering the complaint of the Christian who says, What is religion supposed to be, but the will of God? And what is the will of God, but decent behaviour? And we can try for that, God or no God. That was the bored Christian's complaint. And what was the matter with it? Simply that God's love for us goes infinitely beyond wanting us to be terribly decent by common standards. He wants to make us like himself. It is this infinite care of God for our perfection which above all breaks upon us in the silence. This is the truth: this is what makes us not just a bit disappointed with ourselves, but heart-broken to be what we are. We see God and we see ourselves in a single moment. But though it is sad to see ourselves it is far more joyful to see God, and to trust him who loves us, even as we are.

Maybe you will take the opportunity to attend one of these short retreats arranged for members of the University in the coming season of Lent and especially just after term. If anyone wishes to be put in the way of such an opportunity he need only tell us. But no one needs to wait for that opportunity to arrive. It is excellent to go into retreat but it is much more important to have the habit of re-treating all the time, of making that hole in the busy surface of life which lets through the supernatural light. The essence of it is simply to clear time and hold it clear—until the clock strikes I will keep quiet and let God's truth have my thoughts, and, as often as my mind wanders, return. I suppose I shall begin by reading some verses of scripture, or a list of my friends' names, or recall what my present life is supposed to be about; or just tell myself what God is. But I must give my thoughts to God and believe that he will en-lighten me. It may be dry, and not at all amusing, but I shall be wiser, and I shall know God. And for heaven's sake if you have for-gotten how to pray or never found out, take advice. The place is crawling with parsons, is it not? This is what we are for.

A religion which was primarily personal would not be Christianity: the main expression of Christian faith will remain social action and the corporate praise of God. But if we do not make these holes in the web of life, and look through, we shall risk to lose the Majesty we claim to adore, and the love we profess to share and to serve.

And so, the resolution which may be most vital for you in approaching Lent (and it wouldn't do you any harm to begin, being a good one, even on Septuagesima) is just to secure your times of prayer, and see that they are genuine openings of the window into heaven.

COMMEMORATION OF
CHARLES LINNELL 1915–1964

—preached in Keble College Chapel

A man said to me the other day that he did not find himself believing in the life to come. It is not, he said, like believing in God. God is somehow just there. The life to come isn't just there.

The man who made this observation had really nothing to be worried about. God is an object of immediate faith: for we are dealing with him, or rather he is dealing with us, the whole time. And so, for those who have faith, to live is to believe in God, for as often as they attend to God, they live their belief.

The life to come is not like that: how could it be? It is a future, not a present reality. We do not normally feel it in our environment, nor in our bones. It is the object of hope, rather than of faith. But, as I said, that is no cause for worry. When we call future life our hope, rather than our faith, we are not saying that we only half believe in it. We are merely admitting that it is a future, not a present reality.

What I have said is true, so far as it goes, but it is not absolutely the last word. There are bridges and contacts between earth and heaven, which bring heaven into the present, and allow faith to touch it. Of these the strongest and most evident for Christians is the person of Jesus Christ. Those who look towards Jesus Christ are looking towards one who has made himself for our sakes what we are to become, that is, a man in heaven, a man in glory. So if your faith can put out any sort of hand to reach Christ, you are touching the heart of heaven, and having present contact with what you are, by his mercy, to become hereafter yourself.

Another bridge over the gulf is the dear man who was here with us yesterday, and today is gone from us. About this I will not be ashamed to say something massively simple. The liking we have for a man who has died is all the reason we need for belief in his immortality. For if our dull hearts have seen something to love in a man, which we hate to be without, how much more has the all-knowing heart of God seen something to immortalise! After all, there is no ground whatever for the hope of immortality, except the love of God. And where even we can love, what do you think God can do?

So a dear man who has died is not only a proof of the good providence which shaped him, he is also a token of immortal hope. Our affection *feels* him to be there: his creator's love *makes* him to be there. When we dwell with affection on the person of our friend, we are looking (as well as we can) through the eyes of God and there is no better thing we can do here in our chapel. Charles Linnell might not have agreed with us in thinking that we should be well employed, looking at *him*. He would most emphatically have agreed that the best way to find the heart of God is to trust our own best affections, whatever we are looking at.

If you were simply to go away and gossip about him to one another, that might be the most effective plan for calling up the man dear to God, and dear to us. But I suppose the conventions of the pulpit must be respected: I cannot just give you a string of anecdotes. So what shall I say about him?

Charles Linnell was at once the most parsonical and the least parsonical of men: and perhaps if we can clear up that paradox, we shall have got hold of something. I have just read a piece of painful self-analysis in a parson's trade-journal called *Theology*. The writer declares that the souls of the clergy are devastated by a guilt-complex. Ashamed of their own feebleness, and sensitive to the contempt of mankind, they bid for their own and their neighbours' respect by an endless show of official activity, and an endless display of professional consciousness. They cannot be important; they are resolved to be different. They cannot be saints; they are determined to be martyrs. Well, if that is what you mean by 'parsonical', that wasn't Charles, was it? In that sense of 'parson', Charles wasn't a parson: he was a man. But then you can no more be a man in general, than you can be a dog in general: every dog is of some breed or other and every man has his place and calling. It was as native to Charles to be a parson as it is native to a foxhound to be a foxhound. He was enormously human, enormously alive to his whole human environment: but he saw it from the place where he actually was, his parson's place. For him to talk about his job was to talk about his world; they were the inside and the outside of the same thing. He was most happy in his calling, because it was a better excuse than any other for knowing everyone and everything; he was a sort of friendly old spider, who sat in the middle of a web of gossamer, the threads radiating in all directions—whom didn't they touch? One never came to the end of his contacts and connections.

To return for a moment to my writer in the magazine, the parson scourging his own professional back: he says that the deep-seated cause of parsonical futility is a practical disbelief in God. These men think they've got to work a spell, and put it over on mankind: or they think they've got to organise men into being Christians. As though God were the sleeping-shareholder and they were the executives! Now Charles had the secret of exercising influence. And what is that? Never to do it! The most he would do was to put himself unobtrusively in someone's way: he left himself about, so to speak. The rest lay with Providence.

I don't know whether you remember his preaching about Providence. It was one of his subjects. He had the most simple and assured belief that events are in the hand of God. As you know, the theoretical case for such a belief is very difficult to make out. Perhaps it is best just to say that God can use and does use for his glory everything that happens, however unhelpful it seems, where people trust him. The best evidence for Charles's belief in providence was not his preaching: it was his practice. No need to plan, plot or contrive. Be everyone's friend, and leave the rest to God. If people ask your opinion, tell them the truth; if they ask your advice, give it. Be ordinary. Be yourself. Then just see what God will do.

There is another secret of influence, which was also his, and that is to receive as much as you give. He took us into East Anglia the summer before he died: the country where he had grown up, and where he had exercised his ministry, partly in country parishes, partly in Gresham's School. We were astonished by the universal affection with which he was received, and especially by the protective quality of this affection. Of course he was ill, and could not live long: so people were concerned about him. But it was not only that. They saw him as a man who depended on them, a poor bachelor who needed to be cherished. He needed them just as much as they needed him. If you feel that Charles wanted and liked you, you are perfectly right. He thought that the most sincere way to thank God for his good gifts was to take them with both his hands. He wanted what anyone could give him. He had a rich delight in the world, and in his fellow men.

If you ask why Charles was a bachelor I believe the answer is that he was the only child of his parents and that he was strongly attached to them. By the time they grew old and died he had already learned to find such a deep and wide satisfaction in the personal side of his work, that he carried on as he was. One cannot conceive of his being celibate on any grounds of theory. And yet he was led by God's Providence into exactly that position which St Paul defended theoretically: the unmarried Christian looks after the Lord's business, how to please the Lord. St Paul knew how few men are capable of such simple-mindedness; and of the few who are, perhaps some of the most successful are those who wander into it almost without knowing it; as I suppose happened to Charles. He just found himself absorbed in people, and in all sorts of aspects of God's endlessly enthralling world.

He was celibate, he was certainly not ascetic. He might admire, he could not find congenial the religion which spurns the earth and soars away into ecstasy. His personal religion, to judge by such signs as we saw, was very laical, ordinary and down-to-earth. He just performed cheerfully and sincerely the sort of religious acts we all do half-heartedly or remorsefully. I do not wish to condemn the monkish type of religion; but more relevant to us, surely, is the example of a faith which finds the whole stuff of common life its natural sacrament. So much was this so, you could easily ask yourself, Is this a Christian, or just a very nice man? Did he himself ever quite know where pastoral activity stopped, and where friendship began? I am inclined to believe that he did not know where the line came, and what's more, that he would have felt there was something terribly wrong, and (so to speak) indecent, in being aware of any such line at all.

I was mentioning his simple belief in the Providence which can turn the chances of life to good effect, and I have said that his life illustrates his faith in this article better than his preaching could do. But I have not yet mentioned the most striking example of the principle at work. This was, of course, the deadly illness which drove him to resign his parish and brought him among us. He said himself that these two years were the most fruitful and happy of his life. It would be easy for a man, knowing he had a short time, to frustrate himself in the scramble greatly to enjoy, or greatly to achieve. Just to live under such conditions in fruitful serenity is great virtue, or rather, it is a divine grace. And we know what a blessing God made it to us.

You will not be content with what I have said about so dear a man, nor am I content with it. But if it has led you to think of him, and to thank God, my speech will not have been entirely in vain.